Manifesting 101 & Beyond

Manifesting 101 & Beyond

How to Get What You Want Without Goofing it Up First!

Based on the Popular Electronic Newsletter
Including Guest Authors within the Field

Susan James
susanjames.org

Writers Club Press
New York Lincoln Shanghai

Manifesting 101 & Beyond
How to Get What You Want, without Goofing it Up First!

Writers Club Press
an imprint of iUniverse, Inc.

For information address:
iUniverse
2021 Pine Lake Road, Suite 100
Lincoln, NE 68512
www.iuniverse.com

ISBN: 0-595-14414-4

Printed in the United States of America

To all of the Golden Chocolate Covered Ice Cream that has come into my life to make it more gracious and bountiful, I dedicate this book.

Susan James

*There are no rules, no boundaries, no limits,
other than those self-imposed and self-inflicted.*

Susan James

Contents

Foreword xiii

Having Your Cake and Eating It Too! 1

How I Manifested My Desire: The Parrot Story 3

17–34–68 Second Corner—Tools for Creating! 5

Tool to Help You Focus for 17 Seconds 6

Notice What You Notice! 7

How Do You Get What You Want? Ask!
Period—and Do Not Change Your Mind! 8

Financial Abundance or Financial Lack:
Which One Are You Resonating? 10

How I Manifested My New Computer 13

17–34–68 Second Corner—Tools for Creating! 15

Notice What You Notice! 16

Make Your Dreams Come True; Daydream Your Life Away! 17

Being Good Enough to Stop Overdoing It 20

Learning How the Universe Works—from Geese 23

17–34–68 Second Corner—Tools for Creating! 25

Notice What You Notice! 26

Definitions: Law of Manifesting, Attraction and Allowing 27

Manifesting My Dream Home 28

17–34–68 Second Corner—Tools for Creating! 32

Notice What You Notice! 33

Increasing the Probabilities of Getting What You Want 34

A Beginner at Manifesting, I Wrote It, I Got It! 36

17–34–68 Second Corner—Tools for Creating! 38

Following Your Heart; But Is It Worth It? 40

Transforming Undesirable Habits 42

Summoning Financial Freedom 45

17–34–68 Second Corner—Tools for Creating! 48

How I Manifested a Subdivision 49

17–34–68 Second Corner—Tools for Creating! 52

What Is a Manifestation, Anyway? 53

So How Are You Doing? 55

Making the Decision to Feel Good 57

Deciding What Is Truth 59

On Letting Go… 60

The Difference Between "Needing" & "Wanting" 61

What Does Love Have to Do with Money? 63

Seek and You Shall Find 66

How Do You Enter the Door of Abundance? 67

Trust…But Can You Really Trust It? 68

Molding Energy & Using Your Inner Being/Higher Self 70

Manifestation of Our Farm 71

Write Before You Call! 76

Why Go to All the Trouble? Maybe It's All a Joke! 77

Manifesting Your Desires 79

Trusting Your Impulses 81

Can Asking Include Pain? 84

Burger King & Manifesting 86

One Foot In and One Foot Out—What Will You Miss? 87

And Something Else 89

Turning Things around 90

Loving Allowance 91

Schools of Thought 92

It Just Doesn't Make Sense 94

Introduction to the Beyond Phase 103

Must We Meditate to Hear Our Higher Selves/Spirit? 104

What Happens to Your "Thought" When You Are Done with It? 106

The Wisdom Loft 107

Needles or Noodles 108

Reminder: The Dudd!_The "Do/Un-Do Dance" 109

The "How to" of Getting What You Want Is Changing! 110

The $3,000 Story 112

Have You Found Your Magic Wand? 114

Abundance, But How? 115

Take Money Away! 117

Wake Up! Your Creating! 119

The Wisdom Loft 122

Mohammed Ali & My Boyfriends 123

It Just Falls at My Feet! (More On My Manifesting Story) 125

The Wisdom Loft 127

The Mechanics of Spirit—Part One 128

The Mechanics of Spirit: Part Two—The Handshake 131

The Wisdom Loft—So, What's the Difference? 133

Your Absolute Power: The Handshake 'How-To' 134

Intent Given for Your Higher Self 136

A Question of Rightness 137

The Sword in The Stone/Intent 139

Thought Form=Action & Energy=Emotion 141

The Wisdom Loft (Peace over Fear) 143

Ever Had a Teacher Give You the Answers? 144

Your Higher Self Has Your Answers, But... 147

The Wisdom Loft (More Peace Over Fear) 149

Amazing Things Happen in Flow 150

Thoughts, Thought Forms, Thresholds 153

The Wisdom Loft 155

The Trick to Getting What You Want 156

The Law of Attraction...Works...
The Law of Manifesting...Works... 158

Do You Want to Get Your Dream Back? 159

Inside the Box vs. Outside the Box 161

What is a Vortex, and What Does It Have to Do with Your Desires? 163

When They Ask 165

Un-Stucking to Move Forward 166

The Basics of Feeling Good: Getting Back There 167

Afterword 169

Contributions, Resources, Acknowledgments 171

Biographies 173

Foreword

It gives me great pleasure to have been asked to write the forward for this book. I have worked with Susan over these past months, and all I can say is that she is a master whom I respect greatly. I have watched in awe at how motivated and graceful she is in getting to the next stage of growth. Susan has become one of my very dearest and closest friends. I have so very much enjoyed working with her on this, and many other projects.

This book is about Angels and God and Universal forces. It's about using the science and magic of the Universe and integrating it into our own experiences for a joyful and peaceful existence.

We all decipher for ourselves what our reality is. In this time in history, these "new age" beliefs, which by the way are really "old age" beliefs and have been around for centuries, we are beginning to understand as a mass that no one else can create in another's reality. You are the only one who can create your life experience, and this book shows examples of others' experiences and their perspectives and how they realized their own dreams.

It has been my experience that perspective is so much a part of the end result of how our life really is. This book can help change your perspective, or it can just be fun to read!

And now without further ado, I present to you the woman who made all this possible, Susan James and Manifesting 101, the Book.

Enjoy!

Trixi Summers

1

Having Your Cake and Eating It Too!

(by Susan James)

Let's get to the point; what do I know about "manifesting" that makes me think I can write about it and offer information to others?

This is what I know: Previously, I was professionally and financially successful in several careers, some I created from scratch. I had the toys, the boats the this, the that…But I always was driven to want more.

So with each new career, there was always another endeavor that I was "working" on when I wasn't "working." Why was I doing all this "work?" Well, to get MORE—of course!

The belief at that time was that more work equals more money. Work smarter and harder; make more money. What I was getting was struggle, overwhelmness in the "busyness" of the work activity, more money—but spending more money to keep the business going. More money, less time. Less time to play and have fun. What the heck am I "doing" all of this "doing" for?

Finally, I said "NO MORE;" there has to be another way. There has to be another way to the freedom and joy that I desire. There has to be another way to the absolute freedom, to be and do and have whatever I want, which I knew massive amounts of money would bring.

I "felt" like there was another way, an easier way, I just did not know what is was, but I did start asking some big questions. Who did I know of that was living a full and abundant life, was getting all they desired, and living a life of comfort and ease? Who did I know?

Well, I did not know anyone living who fit this description, I knew some successful people, but mostly they were overwhelmed with it all. That was not what I wanted.

So who did I know? The names I came up with were all dead.

But the one thing these folks all said was "Hey! You can do more, and better than me." Let me teach you. So I began the search—and the information began flooding into my life.

I found that I could have all of my dreams come true, through love and joy, and not struggle and pain, as I had been "taught" previously.

So I began "unlearning" what I had already learned, and replacing that with new techniques that I had never even heard of. What has been the result so far? I no longer work for corporate America. I no longer work frantically 18 hours a day for my dreams to come true. I have no more negative momentum in my life of any kind.

I am in this incredible stream of absolutely everything that I consider to be good just flowing to me with ease. I do exactly what I want to do with my days. Each day is full of fun, passion and contentment. Some days I am thankful for the contentment, to balance the exuberance that I feel!

Money flows to me easily and effortlessly. My relationships are all going great, and I am in excellent health.

And the Dreams that I have set forth for myself—I get reinforcing signs and signals daily that they are coming together, and guess what, I don't even have to "push" them along to make them happen. They are just coming to me.

And what new skills and tools have I developed to live this wondrous life that I live?

I have studied, and continue to do so, the Laws of Attraction, The Laws of Allowing, and the sweet Laws of Deliberate Creation.

Within these Laws is also the law of accelerating acceleration, where what you want and the delivery of your desires move faster and faster towards one another until the manifestation pops!

So what are these Laws and how do you use them? These Laws are about "having your cake and eating it too." You'll have to stay tuned to find out how.

End

2

How I Manifested My Desire: The Parrot Story

(by William Barnes)

I am the richest man I know who as of yet has not a dime to his name! If my "wealth" continues, I will continue manifesting everything I need and want and it won't cost me a thing but a walk in the Sonoran Desert to ask.

I live in a very rural area of Arizona and very literally do not have any neighbors for miles. Though I own a very small plot of land, the surrounding area is also "mine" to explore and enjoy. It is here that I do my best praying.

For instance, I prayed for the best possible publisher for my book "I Built the Titanic: Past Life Memories of a Master Shipbuilder." As luck would have it, my publisher came looking for me rather than vice-versa. But that's another story, for another article.

I love exotic birds, especially parrots. I have a Jenday Conjure named Sammi, who is my constant companion. Now "conjures" are rascally and lovable, but though they can learn some words they are not very good talkers. That's why I've always wanted an African Grey Parrot. They're the best talkers in the world, next to people. African Greys also cost upwards of $2,000 dollars or more, cage and all. I don't happen to have that kind of money in my back pocket, so off I go into the desert to pray.

"Look, Universe..." I usually am very direct. "I like birds. You know that! I really, really want an African Grey." (I am putting a lot of emotion into my words and my desires.) "I want a young, healthy, friendly African Grey that I can afford to have, and I want it to like me. I want to be able to have it in the best possible way." I tell the Universe my parameters. It's like going on search mode on the web. But here, I have to be careful! I have to be specific about what I want and how I want it. I end my prayer with, "The best possible way." That covers anything I may have left out.

If you allow me to digress a moment, I knew someone who prayed for a red sports car. She won it! But it never ran right. She forgot to stipulate dependable. See what I mean?

Back to the parrot. Some weeks later, late one night, I received a call from a cousin in Texas. His fiancee had an African Grey. She could no longer give the bird the attention it needed. He asked "would you like to have it?" He even offered to pay the cost of shipping the bird, cage and all. My only expense was the trip to the Phoenix Airport to pick up a year-and-a-half-old, certified healthy bird, with cage, two months of food and all the toys an active bird could want. Can I cook or what? The point is so can you.

Here's how:

1) Know what you want

2) Know how you want it and express a strong, positive emotion about it. When I do that, I feel as if I'm being picked up from behind. That's when I know I got the Universe's attention.

3) Don't beat around the bush with the Universe by being humble and saying: "Oh, please help humble little me." *Say what you want, Period.*

4) Always, always ask for what you want to happen in the best possible way, with no conditions or "small print."

5) Sit back and wait. Let it go. The Universe has heard you.

So be careful what you pray for. You'll get it!

[1]Read more about Bill in the Biography.

End

---

[1] *Editors note: Bill is on the cover of the December 1998 issue of FATE magazine, with Sammi on his shoulder!*

3

17–34–68 Second Corner—Tools for Creating!

(by Susan James)

"Every 17 seconds of pure thought is equal to 2000 hours of *action*"[2] From Abraham-Hicks Publications. Paraphrased meaning: You have done more in attracting to you what you desire by "thinking/visualizing" about it for 17 seconds than you could by going out and applying 2000 hours of action. (User friendly: what you think is what you get!) You can also UNDO that work by thinking *it won't happen* or *when will it come*, or *it's not here*, thoughts for 17 seconds!
End

. $17\,sec = 2000\;hrs\;of\;action$

---

[2] *From Abraham-Hicks Publications. Web-site: http://www.abraham-hicks.com, J&E Hicks, San Antonio, TX*

4

Tool to Help You Focus for 17 Seconds

(by Susan James)

9–3–9 EXERCISE

1. With your dominant hand, write a one sentence affirmation or prayer of something you want.

2. Write it 9 times.

3. Write it 3 times with your non-dominant hand.

4. Write it 9 times with your dominate hand.

You will notice, especially when writing with your "other hand," how focused you are, and it happens to be MORE than 17 seconds![3]

End

---

[3] *This exercise was paraphrased from the Web-site of Jeanie Marshall, Empowerment Consultant, Marshall House—http://www.mhmail.com—A great site!*

5

Notice What You Notice!

(by Susan James)

As you become more clear on what you are wanting, pay attention to how the Universe communicates to you. The wonder of the Universe supports you in many ways—license plates, billboards, songs, pictures—they are meant to tell you something, but you have to watch and expect to see them. As the Universe knows you are listening, it sends you more and more evidence! And if you're not sure, ask the Universe to show you how you are doing!

6

How Do You Get What You Want? Ask!
Period—and Do Not Change Your Mind!

(by Susan James)

The following two articles, one by Carol James and a follow-up article by William Barnes which appears as the second story in this book (The Parrot Story), are so good and such great examples. Both of their articles are about the Law of Manifesting, which is also the Law of Attracting.

It is all so very simple, and "we" have to get better at catching ourselves at making it hard. Once we begin to "get it"—things, circumstances and conditions all begin dropping into our lives with ease; yes, ease.

Although you may be already involved with some of the principles discussed here, we all "need" to be reminded from time to time of some simple facts: *We can trust our "feelings." If it does not "feel" good, then move away from it. If it "feels" good, then you are moving in the direction to attract more of what you want to you. (This is molding energy for our benefit and advantage)*

Minor but Major example: I was sitting at my computer screen one morning, and nothing was going "right." Nothing was clicking. I felt myself begin to get tense, frustrated, and clogged up! (I could blame it on the Holiday food, not getting my walks in, and my cold and fever—OR…)

At that moment, I had a choice. I could stay at the computer and try and "push" things along, hoping something would get better, or I could just STOP and go do something else until I felt better.

What I know now, that I did not know years ago, is that when I feel good, I attract more of what makes me feel good into my life. If I feel bad and any emotion associated with that, then I begin attracting more stuff that makes me feel bad. It is more than simply just changing our mood. It's understnding what changing our space has to do with our dreams coming true or not.

So what does this have to do with ASKING? We simply ask, or claim, or tell the Universe what we want. When we are "asking" we are feeling good, because we are thinking and feeling about something that we want! We ask with our "vibration." We are "asking" all of the time with our thoughts and feelings.

The Universe responds to our "feelings/emotions" and gives us more of what we are emoting.

As Bill mentioned in his first article, this is not a whimper. It is claiming what is rightfully ours. We are the Universal Force, and it backs us up, but we have to tell it what we want! Then let the Law of Attraction do the "work."

What do you want? Tell the Universe. Then what else do you want? Carol has a lot to say on this, so read it well!

ASK AND IT IS GIVEN; JUST DON'T CHANGE YOUR MIND!

> *ASK, ASK, ASK, TELL, TELL, TELL, CLAIM, CLAIM, CLAIM!*
> *ITS ALL "ASKING" TO THE UNIVERSE!*

This, my wonderful friends, is about Molding Energy. "We" will have lots more to say on that, you betcha!

My best to you
Susan

7

Financial Abundance or Financial Lack: Which One Are You Resonating?

(by Carol James)

I've noticed that there are many people who feel they lack sufficient money to be completely happy. Yet in their wanting of money, they frequently think about the fact that they don't have enough money and about what that lack is preventing them from having, doing or being, and those very thoughts of lack are preventing them from moving forward towards financial abundance.

A paradox for sure: Don't have enough money, want more money, don't have enough money, want more money...A no-win deal, because every time they notice that they don't have enough money, they resonate with lacking money instead of having money. So they do a focus wheel, visualization, meditation or some other ritual around having money, and they resonate with having money until the next bill or expense or purchase they want shows up, and they are reminded that they don't have enough money, so they flip back to resonating with lack.

One can never get to the place of having more money while thinking about not having enough money. Thoughts of financial abundance must be held consistently (not wavering back and forth between abundance and lack) and one must believe (or trust) that all is well, no matter what. Although for many, I understand that this is easier said than done.

So how can one consistently resonate (holding one's tone) with financial abundance, when the current reality of their life says otherwise? For me, I found that the first step was simply to stop thinking about what I don't have and to make a list of all that I do have. At the end of most days, I review all that

I have accomplished and all good things that have happened, no matter how minuscule. That keeps my focus on abundance, which begets more abundance (thought expands).

The next step is that once I think about something I want, I let it go completely. That means that I don't think about how I am going to get it (I trust that my Big U will guide me to do whatever is necessary on my part) or about when it's going to come (it will come when it is time to come) or wonder why it hasn't come yet, which would flip me into lack and doubt. Sometimes my desires will attract stuff that is sort of what I asked for, but not exactly, so I will throw it back and spend some thoughts fine-tuning my request, then resend it. Sometimes I can tell when I am not resonating in harmony with having that which I desire, which is the cause of its delay. But I never doubt that my desires will come to pass eventually, when my thoughts and feelings are aligned with having them.

Next, I trust that my Big U will provide all that I desire—when it is needed. This was a big shift for me, because I used to think that I had to have it weeks or months before I needed it, then I would worry that it wouldn't come on time (fear-doubt). Of course I had no evidence to support this fear-worry-doubt, because I have always been provided for when I needed it, even when I didn't have a clue who would provide it or how it would come. Now I stop worrying about the future, staying focused on my "now," and in my "now" I have plenty of abundance. That's not to say that I don't want more abundance—financial and otherwise—but my abundance continually expands as I focus more and more on the abundance I already have in my life.

The last thing is that I spend all my time focused only on what I love to do or what I am inspired to do (although I can't think of when I'm inspired to do something I don't love). In each moment, I am mindful of whether I am flowing or struggling with what is before me. If I sense that I am struggling, bored, or stalled, I stop working on that project and find something else that feels better. If I can't find something that feels better, then I know that I am experiencing a thought or belief-block, and I will step back to ponder my current state of beingness. My blocked states last only as long as it takes me to recognize which aspect of my thinking has caused the block.

In this way, regardless of my financial state, I always do and be exactly what I am wanting and what feels good. To me, feeling good is the goal, not having more money. So, whether or not I am able to buy something has no bearing on my state of feeling good. In my release of not needing money before I can be happy, I've freed up my energy toward having money, which has allowed money to always show up exactly when I want it.

Read more about Carol in the Biography Section.

8

How I Manifested My New Computer

(by William Barnes)

Well, I did it once again! No, I didn't manifest another parrot. Rather, I managed to "buy" a brand new computer without spending a dime. Impossible? Not when you practice what we preach in Manifesting 101.

Three weeks ago my old computer literally burned up. In fact, right after I finished the parrot story my computer struck a cyber-berg and went down with all hands.

Now this is the death knoll to an author with a new book just published. How was I going to answer my E-mail or investigate sales opportunities?

Well, back I go into the desert to talk to the Universe. If you recall, I said that expressing emotion in your requests is important. Believe me, emotion was NO trouble to an author deprived of his "pen." The Universe and I had a nice chat. I was sure I had everything I needed expressed.

I walked back to my house. As I walked in, my friend, Dale who rents a room from my wife and I asked what the burning smell in the house was. "My old computer," I answered. "And I was just out praying for a new one."

Dale then shared with me his own problems. He really needed to get online himself, because he felt it would help his acrylic art business. No computer in the house was beginning to affect all of us.

All of a sudden Dale said, "I've got an idea! Why don't I buy or lease a computer? I can take it off as a business expense, and I'll let you borrow it as much as you want."

I in turn agreed to deduct a portion of his rent. Well, we ordered the computer, and the rest is history—except…

Do you remember in my last article I stated the importance of being specific? Well, I wasn't this time. The computer has great speed, a large SDRAM (160mg) AND I was also able to find a local Internet server to cut down on my phone bills, but I forgot to specify a sound card. I'll have to deal with that shortly.

Nonetheless, I'm back on line and I haven't spent a cent!

Bill

Read more about Bill in the Biography!

9

17–34–68 Second Corner—Tools for Creating!

(by Susan James)

Question: How long has it been since you wrote a letter to God/Universe, or yourself, expressing what you want for your life? Just sitting down and doing this, you begin to change "old habits"; you begin to "unlearn." Notice how you are "feeling" as you write only about what you "want," NOT what you "don't want." This "feeling" is vibrational "asking" to the Universe.

Your choice here is to continue to "toil and strain" for what you want, or just sit down and write a letter. Then wonder begins…Is it as simple as "that?" Yes, but you must "learn the new skill" of not "changing your thoughts" back to "it won't happen." STOP changing your mind. The Universe always says "YES." It does not care if it shows up in your experience as positive or negative; it simply responds to the message you send through your thoughts and emotions.

So notice how are you "feeling" today, because that's what you'll get MORE of!

10

Notice What You Notice!

(by Susan James)

"Teach yourself the Law of Attraction, then you won't need Faith; you have Knowledge that anything you focus upon Will Be."[4]

---

[4] *From Abraham-Hicks/El Paso 1998 (audio) Abraham-Hicks Publications. Web-site: http://www.abraham-hicks.com, J&E Hicks, San Antonio, TX*

11

Make Your Dreams Come True; Daydream Your Life Away!

(by Susan James)

Make your dreams come true; daydream your life away! Yeah, BUT is it practical, logical, and reasonable? Most reading this are by now "adults," and most I would speculate have grown up with learning to do things backwards, which is how we have been "taught." It's no one's "fault" really, it just "is," until it "isn't" for "you" anymore.

I have always been open-minded, enthusiastic, and optimistic about life—mine especially—never mind what it "looked like." What I came to know is that those are wonderful traits to have, but it is not enough to make your dreams comes true. Maybe you will reach some of your goals, but you may get there in pain and struggle or in ways that you really don't like, and there is an easier and more fun way. I mean, what if you could "really" create abundance and prosperity in your life by doing what you "really" LIKED to do! (Imagine that!)

I finally came to know, and to use, two important tools that I have had all along but did not know how to use them properly. These tools are just like the tools of "smell, taste, sound, touch, and sight." We know how we use these tools. I won't waste your time explaining that. The "old" tools that became "new" to me are my "feelings" and my "imagination."

We use our imagination all the time, almost in every moment. We either imagine something past, present or future. When we learn to use our imagination on "purpose," we get more of what we want in our lives and less of what we don't want. The other choice is not to use our imagination on "purpose," and we end up just "banging around" and adjusting and reacting to what comes our way. This usually shows up in the form of pain and struggle, and I know you know what I mean!

When I learned and gave myself permission just to "ponder" on purpose what I wanted for my life, I immediately put my "daydream maker" to work. As I practiced more frequently "thinking" (imagining) how I wanted my life to be and things and situations I wanted, the more good stuff just started showing up! Whoda thunk it? It's okay to imagine what I want and let the circumstances unfold for it to happen!

You will read real experiences in the upcoming essays of Manifesting 101 from people who finally went "Okay, I get it!" And they have received things they wanted, just by thinking and daydreaming about it and not changing their mind (thoughts) about it happening!

The other tool I learned to use on purpose was finally realizing that it is *ok* to trust my own feelings! WO, that was a biggy! You mean I can trust how I feel and the emotion that it gives me to guide me?

So that became simple. If it feels good, do it; if it doesn't, don't. Can you believe I even wrote that? "If it feels good, do it." When you "feel **good emotions**," it is the Divinity within you telling you, "Yes, you are on the path." When something does not "feel" good, then you are not connected as closely to that path where all things which YOU consider to be good will just flow to you!

Gerald G. Jampolsky, MD wrote in his book "*Love is Letting Go of Fear*":

> "*I am finding that when personal guidance has established the goal, (the cart), All I need do is keep that goal firmly in my mind and the means (the horse) will take care of itself.*" "*Most of us expend so much energy in trying to find the means that we lose sight of the goal.*"

Do you see, with "your" tool of sight, what he is saying here? "Keeping the goal firmly in my mind..." He is using his imagination, his thoughts; he is thinking about what he wants; HE IS NOT THINKING ABOUT THE HORSE, or how it will come to him, he just keeps thinking about what he wants!

And then there is Darryl Anka, who writes in his book, *Blueprint for Change*,

> "*As long as you understand that you are doing what you are doing, that you are expressing the desires you are expressing through joy, though love, though service, through integrity, there is nothing, nothing, nothing, that the Universe will withhold from you.*"... "*If you know you have*

the capability of imagining what you would like to be, understand, that YOUR ABILITY TO IMAGINE WHAT YOU WOULD LIKE TO BE IS YOUR ABILITY TO BE THAT PERSON, that version of you."

You must know that the Vastness, the Greatness of the Universe, of God, is behind you, with you and in you. Learn to use the tools properly and on purpose, and the entire quality of your life and the lives of others you care for, and the quality of your contribution to everything and everyone that exists simply expands and grows and develops in heaps, bounds, in joy, easy and fun ways!

Imagine that. You can daydream your life, away. Imagine that!

My Best Love to All,
Susan

P.S. If you are "feeling a little tense" about this "feelings and imagining" stuff, just ponder this: God is Love, and God is Joy. When you sit and think about what you want for your life, how do you "feel" in that moment? If you feel joy and warmth and love and good, is that of your God?

12

Being Good Enough to Stop Overdoing It

(by Tom Haskins)

I've gotten good at manifesting lately. That gives me a bunch of things to say about how easy it is. Yet while I was trying to get good at manifesting, hearing how easy it is wasn't helping me. I felt left out, like I was missing the point or was wrong somehow. In hindsight, I'd say I was trying too hard to be good at manifesting and had to overdo it to get to the stage of letting go. It seems we have to under-do manifesting to feel compelled to overdo it, too, then simply be good at manifesting.

I received an inner prompting to start a daily gratitude journal last September. I faithfully listed incidents and experiences I appreciated several times each day. Prior to that, I had been grateful for outstanding things that happened. The journal got me expressing gratitude for lots of small and repetitive things. I saw I was making the transition from "doing the gratitude thing" to "having an attitude of gratitude," or to "simply being a grateful person."

What we appreciate multiplies in our experience. I wasn't getting the feeling of being "good at manifesting" while I was keeping the gratitude journal. I was overdoing my effort to show gratitude.

In mid November I received another inner prompting to stop keeping the journal. I was told to simply think the thought of "thank you for this" at any moment during the day. If I had stopped the journal prematurely, I would have reverted to being "ungrateful" most of the time. That vibration repels desired manifestations. By writing down appreciative thoughts three times a day for three months, I went from under-doing gratitude, to over doing it, to simply being grateful.

Living in gratitude is like being a preheated oven. There is so much that is possible within the realm of possibilities for this vibration. Yet our capability to cook with ease still needs cakes to bake called desires.

I've found I can overdo wanting things, too. When I am trying too hard to want something, it feels like I am talking to myself, and the Universe is not listening. When I am "being good at manifesting," it feels like I am being heard, and things I want show up without "much ado about wanting."

I'll even get inner promptings to want something and it shows up instantly—to show me manifestations come by being open to them, not by doing something to make them come to me. Wanting things simply makes us receptive and appreciative.

I've been teaching college part-time since 1992. I've manifested lots of inspirations for how to make my classes fun to teach and exciting for the learners. I've attracted oodles of appreciation from students and the administration. I've repeatedly realized the truism, "the best way to learn something is to teach it." I've gained a staggering amount of wisdom in this work that feels like playing.

When I started, I over-prepared and wearied myself with "trying to be a good teacher." That process taught me to ease up. I started to see that "I am a good teacher." I still had better ways to teach in my mind that would take more time and bigger budgets to prepare. Most of these improvements involved distance learning, elaborate web sites and self paced instruction. I was in the frame of mind that "I was good, but I could be better." Much of the class scheduling bothered me. My circumstances were "wanted, yet unwanted."

It was a match to my experience of "teaching is getting easier under some adverse conditions," but it was still a struggle for me to be completely satisfied with what I do. The lurking dissatisfaction set me up to overdo my preparation for classes.

The University knows I love to play around with preparing any class I've never taught before, so they just gave me a new one for the seventh time. Usually the inspirations come easily for how to teach it, and I'm off to a running start when the semester starts. This latest course was failing to capture my imagination or come together in my mind. It was time to let go of overdoing how I manifest teaching preparations and to simply being good at manifesting.

Out of nowhere, I got an E-mail from a Broadway producer who had just read something I had written 20 months ago about on-line learning. He then called me from New York, seeking advice about a distance learning class he'd been asked to teach.

In the process of that very uplifting phone call with him, I realized the way I now teach is more effective and motivational than those improvements I could not afford. The Universe sent me a spectacular messenger to get me to be completely satisfied with how I already teach. I went from "struggling to do enough to be satisfied" to simply "being a very good teacher."

Meanwhile, I'm having plenty of other experiences of already "being good at manifesting" with shopping when items are on sale, missing the ill effects of weather changes, getting heating system repairs before I put in a request, catching a TV program I had not heard about, receiving heartwarming E-Mails, and reading books in a perfect sequence. So this oven is hot and the cakes are baking.

The blockages to class preparation vanished. First came inspirations for a major change in grading the students work to take less of my time while enhancing the students ability to appreciate their own efforts. Then came ideas for making the content more visual than ever before and giving students more ways to be proud of their accomplishments.

Then the University called with an emergency, needing me to teach a 3rd class. Last Fall I had told the Department Chair if I ever taught that Strategy Class again, I would cover the topics in a completely different order. That revised sequence came to me in a flood of excitement at 4:00 A.M. two days ago, and I got it all written down before sunup. The time slot is amazingly perfect for me, too. I can hardly wait to start teaching that class and see what a difference it makes to teach this total departure from the textbook.

So consider this. What did I have to do to? Get the respect of a Broadway producer, to lose my resistance to being satisfied, to remove elusive blockages to course prep inspirations, to get a perfectly scheduled opportunity to teach the Strategy class "my way" and to receive a 50% increase in teaching income? Pick up my phone and check my E-mail! After the necessary stage of overdoing gratitude, I've discovered it takes very little doing to be blessed with treats beyond measure.

Simply be good at manifesting in your mind, be grateful in your heart and the Universe will show up like it's throwing a party in your honor.

There is more to know of Tom in the Biography Section!

13

Learning How the Universe Works—from Geese

(by William Barnes)

Here's my version of a Mother Goose story with a REAL Mother goose!

I own a poultry ranch in Gila Bend, Arizona. I raise ducks, chickens, peacocks and geese. By now you've probably figured out that I like birds of all kinds. You can learn a lot from birds, including how the Universe works when we want something.

Gertude is a big white Emden goose that looks almost like a swan. She's gentle as a lamb and likes to "talk" to anyone who'll listen. Recently, Gertrude dug a nest and laid one egg. She covered it up and walked (waddled) away. She did this the next day, too, and the next and the next. Finally, six good-sized eggs were in the nest and she began to sit on them. After a few weeks, the first egg hatched at the same time the last egg hatched. In all, six little goslings were born at the same time. You see, fertile goose eggs stay dormant until they are kept at a certain temperatureabove 97.5 degrees.

The Universe puts out answers to our prayers in much the same way. One situation as part of the answer, is given us here, another there. Finally, everything comes together, and after a time—fruition. It's just that sometimes we get impatient or lose faith in the process and then we make it harder for things to happen.

Were I to touch Gertrude's eggs, she might not go back to them, or worse, I could infect the porous eggs with human bacteria from my hands; then there would be no little goslings. So I have to stand back and wait, no matter how excited I am to see the little critters hatch.

That's why we are instructed to "let go and let God" after we pray for something. By relinquishing control to the Universe, we insure the best! Well, gotta go! I've got six more hungry mouths to feed!

Sincerely,
Bill

Read more about Bill's book in the Biography Section!

14

17–34–68 Second Corner—Tools for Creating!

(by Susan James)

As you begin trusting your feelings more than your intellect in making your decisions and choices, you will still most likely have moments of negative emotion that simply have you "feeling"—well, negative. (Anger, frustration, sadness, fear, lack).

Something that I use, that I mentioned in issue #1, was the 9–3–9 exercise, and I do it both in writing and verbally.

I just write on a piece of paper, "I want to feel good," "I want to feel good," and I say it verbally whenever I feel like I need to. As I have done this exercise, I have almost immediately begun feeling better. You must know that the most important thing any of us can do in each moment is to feel good—to feel joy; for it is there that we are connected to God, the Universe, the All That Is. It is there that all things which we consider to be good will just flow to us.

Doing this as a focused exercise for a minimum of 17 seconds is a powerful exercise, for it combusts into 2000 hours of work/energy "out there."

15

Notice What You Notice!

(by Susan James)

As you learn to ASK the Universe for signs and symbols, "remember" to pay attention, because you WILL get Answers, and you will "feel" that you have been given an answer. Next Step, trust what you "heard, felt, or saw."

16

Definitions: Law of Manifesting, Attraction and Allowing

(by God & The Universe, His/Her playground!)[5]
(by Susan James)

LAW OF ATTRACTION: The most powerful Law in the Universe.
You are a magnet attracting that which you are thinking, and feeling.

As you stay focused and open, your wants, wishes and desires will absolutely under all conditions be yours. *IT IS LAW!*

You create through thought, not through a lot of action.

DELIBERATE CREATION: When you are acting in Joy from thought, it then leads to manifestation inspired to action in joy. You do not "go" and get it. You act in joy and it comes to you. You think your future, your dreams, your wants and desires into being. You see it, you visualize it, you expect it, and it is and will be. You are inspired, guided or led to the perfect action that leads you to, brings about the process, that leads/brings you that which you seek.

LAW OF ALLOWING: You are that which you are, and you are pleased with it. You do not focus on what brings discomfort.

---

[5] *Materials on Law of Attraction, Law of Allowing and Law of Deliberate Creation originally from Abraham-Hicks Materials. Web-site: http://www.abraham-hicks.com, J&E Hicks, San Antonio, TX*

17

Manifesting My Dream Home

(by Sharon Hackleman)
(Sharon Hackleman—Brief Bio)

I live in Soldotna, Alaska with my two daughters, Cherie, 16 and Rachael 12. I am married to an excellent allower, Kent. I got turned onto ABE (Abraham-Hicks) four years ago by my sister Mary and since then I have manifested many things that, before my knowledge of Universal Law, I thought only the other guy could do. I truly have come to know that I can be or do or have anything I want! I have proven this to myself many times, I'd like to share one of those manifestations with you.

Our New Home

Four years ago, my family and I lived in a quaint 800 square foot, one bedroom cabin on an acre of land. We lived there for five years, adding on here and there. It was our first home, and we put our heart and soul into making it livable and comfortable. After about four years, we all began to feel a little cramped and were ready for a larger house. The only thing was I had been ill with pneumonia that year and it had wiped us out financially, as we had no insurance. My husband and I declared bankruptcy and thought because of that we would have to remain in our little cabin until we were able to secure financing, which we were told could take seven to ten years after filing bankruptcy. Hmmmm—drag. We were looking forward to moving up sooner than that; another seven years in this little cabin didn't set well with any of us. Deep in my gut, I knew it would be sooner than that. We would find a way.

That spring, my husband and I decided to take our long-awaited honeymoon to Maui, and it was there that I was turned onto the ABE material. I took to it quickly; I knew that this was one of the reasons I came to Maui. I was intrigued and empowered by what I was hearing. I knew that these tapes held the secrets I had been looking for! My husband wasn't so impressed; he thought Esther was just changing her voice. I remember thinking it didn't matter what anyone thought, this was about ME and how I was going to USE this information. I continued to listen to the tapes daily, and soon I was applying the principles to things such as more money on our paychecks, bills vanishing from records, stuff like that. Now this was pretty damn impressive to me. I would focus on my husband's check being more than we thought it would be and he would end up getting paid the billable rate, rather than his hourly wage, which would add more than $1,000.00 to his two-week paycheck! I knew then that I was dealing with a force that could get me anything I wanted! I tried it out on a few outstanding bills that I could not declare bankruptcy on and PRESTO, they vanished! No trace of them, period. I played with it with my bank account and I gott $1,000.00 extra added onto my deposit! O.K., I was sold; I really can use this energy field to create anything I want. What do I really want? **A NEW HOUSE!**

My husband was beginning to see what was happening and knew it was more than just chance. He was starting to get intrigued, too, but really wasn't into listening to the tapes, although he did listen to me, so I began to show him what the material was about by being an example of it myself. I told him that we could move out of this cabin into a nice new house, even with our financial background. I knew it in my heart, and I was ready to apply the same principles I had learned from ABE to this endeavor.

The road blocks seemed endless, but I remained fix in my focus, and soon we had our little cabin ready for inspection for financing. This was one of the biggest challenges, because it was pieced together and we bought it with owner financing. We were not even sure if it would pass all the codes! We needed to be cashed out so we could purchase our new home. Once again, I maintained my pure focus and FAITH in the principles, and believed it would pass for financing. I took ABE at their word that I could be or do or have anything I wanted; I believed them. I wouldn't entertain any thought that was contrary to our goal. If a thought came up, or a 'what if' popped into my head, I would hear ABE reminding me to keep it clean. There were plenty of reasons for me to think it could not be financed, but I wanted it so badly that I chose to look at the positive points of this experience. Kent and I had purchased the cabin for $25,000.00 and with the improvements we were asking $60,000.00; we only owed $12,000.00 on the note. That was a $48,000.00 cash transaction! O.K. I'm going there, man! It can and will sell, period. **I THANK GOD FOR THE AMOUNT OF FAITH I HAVE. IT WORKS!**

During the selling of our house, I was out looking for the new perfect house. Kent and I had looked at a few, but not able to get financing our selection was unique. We could get owner financing, but the majority of those were dumpy. Kent went back to the slope for his hitch, and I continued to flow on selling our house and looking for the perfect new one. I always knew we would get what we wanted. We had $48,000.00 cash to offer up; someone would listen!

It was just a week later when I called on a house that fit our description to a T! It was a house that was just a year and a half old. The family was going through a divorce and the man couldn't afford the payments any longer. It was an owner finance situation with just $8,000.00 down required. It had three bedrooms, three bathrooms, a garage, over 2100 square feet of living space on a half acre of land! It was right down the street from my youngest daughter's school and the neighborhood was nice. **I WANTED THIS HOUSE!** I knew that this house would be mine. I would make this happen!

I called my husband Kent and he could hear the **STRONG DESIRE** in my voice for purchasing this house. By now, Kent had seen me manifest many things, and his **FAITH** in me was so strong, he was willing for me to finalize the deal without him even seeing the house! That was a cool feeling! This entire dream was unfolding perfectly! Now, I just had to sell our little cabin and get the cash!

We had a nice couple look at it and really want it, but their financing fell through. I remember that night vividly, because I was counting on them to buy it, and that phone call informing me that they couldn't secure financing put me into a place of **EXTREME DESIRE!** I ran to my bedroom and I let out the biggest squeal: **I WANT TO FIND A BUYER FOR MY HOUSE!** I was half crying, half demanding, all kinds of emotions all at once, but I remember **DESIRE** being the strongest! Within a few moments, the phone rang and it was the man who ended up buying the house with a veteran's loan, and the deal was closed within a month! He didn't even quibble about the price! Ta Dah!

Kent and I purchased our big home and felt like we defied all the 'rules' we had been taught, or the restrictions that were supposed to label us after bankruptcy! We did it with great **DESIRE** and strong **FAITH** in these principles. We furnished the home with brand new cream leather couches and glass tables; we paid cash for everything! We felt like we had won the lottery! I would call the bank just to hear my balance! :) After we furnished our new home, we took a family vacation to Disneyland and then to Mexico! The entire time we were on vacation, we basked in the feeling of going home to a brand new house! It was so exciting!

The entire family used the principles of Universal Law to 'seal this deal.' We all used the **DESIRE, FAITH** and a lot of visualization and fantasizing! It was a biggy for us, because we knew we were intentionally 'doing it,' and when you see the manifestation of your deliberate thought, it is a kick in the pants! Pretty much a **POWER TRIP** of the most powerful kind.

18

17–34–68 Second Corner—Tools for Creating!

(by Susan James)

Spend 15 minutes each day "scripting" how you imagine your life to be. Write as though you are living and enjoying it now. Write how you feel as you imagine, how you live your dream.

Then just watch—AND DON'T CHANGE YOUR MIND. The second step is that if out of habits, habits that you have learned, you find yourself saying and thinking, *I want this,*BUT I know it won't happen. Quickly notice what you just did, and undo it. Talk about what you want and why you want it. 17 seconds, 17 seconds, 17 seconds, notice how you feel, as you talk and envision what you want. THAT is what the Universe hears and delivers!

"The most important thing you can do in each moment is to feel good!"

(Thanks Jeff Forte, for that quotation, that sticks with me always & in all ways!)[6]

[6] *Original quotation from Abraham-Hicks, Web-site: http://www.abraham-hicks.com, J&E Hicks, San Antonio, TX*

19

Notice What You Notice!

(by Susan James)

As you learn to ASK the Universe/God for signs and symbols, "remember" to pay attention, because you WILL get Answers, and you will "feel" that you have been given an answer. Next Step, trust what you "heard, felt, or saw."

So one day, I had a long talk and writing period (scripting), with the Universe—about my intentions, my desires, and I was pretty blunt and clear. I also asked to be given signs and symbols to let me know how thing were coming together.

WELL, that next morning on my drive into the office along quiet dark country roads, I saw within short distances of one another *TWO* Christmas Trees, colorfully lit! Now excuse me, but it was almost February! So what did I NOTICE? That this was a sign from the loving Universe of the Gifts to come; yummyness and joy abounds!

20

Increasing the Probabilities of Getting What You Want

(by Susan James)

Question:	*What is the single most important and easiest way to get what you want?*
Answer:	*(choose) (a.) Imagination, (b.) Imagination, (c.) Imagination.*

If you chose imagination, you are "correct." A quotation from Richard Bach's "Illusions:" "Just your imagination? Of Course it's your imagination! Where your "thinking" is, is where your experience is. As you think, so you ARE. To bring anything into your life, imagine it is already there."

He goes on to say, "It does not take faith. Takes Zero Faith. What it takes is imagination…" Since you have imagination as a grain of sesame seed, all things are possible to you. (Tip: Back in Biblical times, they did not have a word for "imagination").

So how do you use this "imagination" to get what you want? First, you must recognize it as a "sensory tool." Just like, touch, sight, hearing, are all sensory tools, they give us information, so does our imagination. It gives us information in the form of "feelings," just like touch, sight, hearing all give us information through our feelings & emotions, which then lead to our experience.

When we use our imagination as a tool, we can build our lives to be more of what we want. We can use it to pay the rent or to purchase a home. We can use it to fall in love, and/or heal ourselves. What we have to do is to get "good" at using it as a tool.

We have to practice using it as a tool. How do we do that? We think about things that we want. We daydream. We picture what we want to happen, and we notice how we feel. If we feel good as we are thinking of something, then the creation process of bringing it to us has begun, automatically.

We push it away by thinking that it won't come. So the practice part is thinking about it always working out the way we want and staying in "that place."

"Don't let a day go by without thinking about what you want." "When we focus on an intention or a goal, imagining that it is already there, the inner self gets set to archive that goal in ways that the conscious mind can't plan or understand" ("Beyond the Winning Streak" by Lynda M. Dahl).

You simply make it easier for the Universe/God to deliver to you your desires by increasing the probabilities. How do you increase the probabilities? Use your imagination!

Oh, and by the way, you can still do it "backwards," which is the way most of us were taught. You know, you go "work, to do, to get…" Your "other" choice is to allow it to just come to you. Manifesting 101, among many things, is about using your imagination for cause and effect, instead of "sweat equity."

21

A Beginner at Manifesting, I Wrote It, I Got It!

(by J. N.)

This subject of manifesting has been fascinating. I tried what I understood of it, writing down what I wanted and why I would get it. I was having a hard time with my Significant Other, feeling unloved and kind of alone; not that there was any real problem, just that he was on a business trip and things hadn't been—mm—flowing between us like they usually are. A misunderstanding a couple weeks ago that was smoothed over, but not settled. That sort of thing, just tight.

I wrote out how loved I am, how my footsteps are so guided that they will lead me to those who will love me and help me on my way, filling my needs—one of which is love—so I have it, and will have it all the more as I learn to take it. (I don't know where all that came from, but its part of what I wrote).

Not 15 minutes later, he called me from overseas to tell me how much he loves me, that I am his only love, that he is investing everything in me, and still kicking himself over losing a past opportunity that we had for me to come live with him, how he wishes he could make that happen now.

I didn't think much about the writing afterwards; I was too busy enjoying the glow from our talk (see me smile...) But a few hours later, I realized what had happened. I'm so impressed. I was feeling a bit skeptical at first. After all, he always loved me. Just—just interesting timing, right?

Uh huh. I was talking with my ex and he told me about something that's going to be getting me 400–500 dollars tomorrow, something I didn't expect, and I realized it had already happened again. I didn't even write out anything about money, I just spent some time thinking about it as something I will be getting, something I can't help but get, feeling excited about it and grateful for getting it—and here it is—and until now, I wasn't the type of person to get money, ever. (It's an odd situation).

Twice in one day, in a matter of a couple hours actually, that's—that's just a bit much for me to call coincidence. I'm just amazed. I didn't think it would be so quick. I'm used to things being subtle, small nudges my way that I am never really sure that I did, you know? Not bad! 15 minutes for professions of undying love and two hours for a few hundred dollars.*L*

I'm so excited, I feel like a kid in a candy store.*Grin*Actually, I feel giddy and tingling.

22

17–34–68 Second Corner—Tools for Creating!

(by Susan James)

Assuming the goal is to help you "visualize" AND to feel good about what you are looking at.

Try this: It is a new one that I have been doing, and it FEELS great!

In a 3-ring binder I put, in plastic hseets, pictures of the following:

A. *Someone whose life I intend on having (Livelihood/Lifestyle).*

B. *Pictures of people, very successful at the "livelihood" that I intend.*

C. *Pictures of the vehicles I intend on having.*

D. *Pictures and pamphlets of the city I intend to have and be and do "in."*

E. *The photo of the home I intend on performing my life and livelihood from.*

What I do with this binder?

EVERY DAY, for 15 minutes, I sit with a cup of coffee and just look at the binder and talk about what I see and how I see myself there. I make up stories. I notice how I am feeling, which is always elation, warmth and gratitude.

Some days I cannot sit doing it, so I walk around with the binder, totally enthralled in what I am anticipating, and it is coming! I know it, I feel it, and part of it already is here!

When I do this early in the day, it sets up my energy for the entire day, which just brings more good stuff to me throughout the day!

Question: Are you willing to do this, this 15 minutes, to completely change your life into what you want it to be like? Once you begin, it becomes habit just to do, and you can't help but want to do it, because you know its coming!

And why do you know it is coming? **IT IS LAW!** *(Law of Attraction)*

23

Following Your Heart; But Is It Worth It?

(by Susan James)

Your heart says "Go," your mind says "Stay." Your heart says "Go for it!" Your mind says, "Are you crazy?" Your heart says "Go," but your institutions (religion, education, society) say "Stay."

Your heart says "Go for it." Your institutions say, "Are you crazy, or just plain stupid and irresponsible?"

How do you choose? Do you choose? Or do you back away? Backing away, is a choice.

How do you choose? You begin by asking yourself some "serious" questions. What do you want? What do you really want? Is what you are currently "doing/being" giving you what you desire for your life?

Assuming you, like most of "us," want "fun, happy, joy, prosperity, love,"do you even believe that you can actually have those things? And that they can come to you with ease?

What do you have to "do" to have this? Follow your heart!

Your heart is divinely connected to that wonderful stream of goodness, of God, of the Universe in its simplicity and complexity.

Your institutions have taught you not to "listen" to this "heartness," and you have been such a good student for over 20, 30, 40, 50, 60 years. You get an "A" for following against yourself, against your heart, against your own wisdom. You have excelled in these institutions. So how do you feel? Are you happy? Are you prosperous? Are you elated and excited about each and every day of your life? Do you even know that this is the way your life "was supposed to go?" Do you know that?

How do you move into that state of "everything going your way" and feeling great about you and everyone in your life, and how do you "get there?"

You get there simply by making a conscious decision about your life. Then, you "work" on changing what you believe about how life works. The Institutions have taught you their ways. HOWEVER, we all have at our use and disposal "Universal and Divine Laws." Some choose to dispose of this fact; that does not change the fact that Universal Law is operating in each moment. If you choose to believe this is "hokey," then it is—for you; for as you "believe," so it is.

If, however, you agree that maybe, possibly, you do not know all that there is to know about how God and the Universe works, then you have some wonderful tools entering your life to use for your own design.

The first step is changing what you believe about how life works, and if you are not yet at this stage, just being a little open to the possibility will begin the process.

To quote my friend Paula Sirois, "How I love when doors fly open as I simply relax and bask in a stream of delightful manifestations of DIVINE LAW!"

An important step in this beginning process is giving you permission to "follow your heart." It is okay to follow your own intuition and guidance. Just ask yourself how you feel, instead of what you think. They are two entirely different perspectives sometimes, especially when your life is not going well, and therein lies the key.

As always—and following my heart, as it is yours.
Susan

24

Transforming Undesirable Habits

(by Carol James)

There is no difference between creating money, self-love, fabulous relationships, fulfilling work or any other thing you can imagine. The key is not in WHAT you want, but rather in how you FEEL about what you want.

Have you ever noticed that things you get easily and quickly are those things that you are not resistant to having or that you are not anxious about how or when you will have them? That is because you allowed them to enter your experience in their own way and in their own time. You didn't get fearful, doubtful, anxious, worried or resistant about having them, about how they would come to you or about when you would have them. You just didn't think much about them at all, except perhaps in that initial moment when you fantasized about having them. You just let it go. *Voila!* You got them.

No matter what you desire to create, the path is always the same. Resonate with "having" and you get; resonate with "not having" and you don't get (at least not getting exactly what you asked for). If you observe yourself feeling or thinking any of the following, then it's a good bet that you are resonating with not having:

Feeling anxious
Feeling nervous
Worrying of any kind
Fretting over details
Fearing that it won't come on time
Fearing that it won't come at all
Wondering when it will come
Wondering if it will come

Questioning whether or not you deserve it
Fearing what will happen if it doesn't come
Freaking out about the consequences of not having it
Feeling panicky, depressed or fearful
Feeling tired, exhausted or frustrated

The most important questions is this: what do you do when you find yourself caught in any undesirable habit of thought? Here are some tips to transform the situation:

Recognize that you are indulging in negative chatter and acknowledge that this is merely an old, worn out habit that just needs to be transformed. If you can catch yourself in the act, then all the better.

Don't beat yourself up for thinking negatively. You weren't born thinking negatively, you were just taught to do that, and no one ever taught you how to think positively, so you have a habit of thinking negatively. No big deal. You've transformed other undesirable habits in your life, haven't you? This is no different. So get busy focusing on how to transform it.

Besides, thinking about what you don't want (thinking negatively) is powerless to give you what you do want. The only thing that can give you what you want is focusing on having what you want.

Find a replacement habit. If you don't want to think negatively, then what do you want? Most likely to think positively, so that's an easy one.

Create an Appreciation Journal. Write about any new things you've found to appreciate, or about exciting miracles that happened, or about neat and heartwarming things that have touched your heart. Anytime you catch yourself thinking negatively, just whip out your Appreciation Journal and reread the entries you've made. That should pivot your thoughts quickly and easily. While you're at it, add a few new entries to your journal. Of course, any other replacement habit will do, as long as it promotes health and well-being.

Take the time to identify the deeper need lying behind the thoughts. For instance, thinking negatively often carries a deeper fear of feeling unlovable or not good enough or afraid of being rejected for making a mistake or any number of self-diminishing or self-doubting thoughts. Ask yourself why you feel or believe that way and why you believe that is true.

For instance, if you feel that you are not good enough, then why not? What facts have you gathered to prove that you are not good enough? And does everyone in the entire world think you are not good enough? And so what if you are not good enough to please SOME people? Who cares about what those people think, anyway, because if they are so judgmental and critical, then why would you want them in your life? Have you ever been good enough? And who said you were? And what does it really mean to be good enough? Good enough for what? What are you prevented from doing or being, if you are considered not good enough? And who started this distorted and fearful game of accusing people of not being good enough? How can you change your way of looking at yourself (or others) to be able to reverse this habit? How do people who feel they are good enough think, feel, speak and behave? What values and ideas do they believe in? What would it take for you to feel like you were good enough? Get the idea?

Be determined and persistent. Thinking negatively about self is a habit of thought and focus, which was taught to us by people within our early environment (i.e., parents, siblings, teachers, etc.). It's probably a habit that's been around for eons, unknowingly being passed from generation to generation. Why is that? Because people don't tend to question the validity, desirability and value of beliefs they hold. Breaking any undesirable habit requires that you be diligent in catching yourself in action doing the undesirable behavior (for instance, putting yourself down) and replacing the old habit with a new one (appreciating all that you have and are). Build up your determination by creating a list of reasons why you want to transform the undesirable habit, listing everything you will gain and the benefits you will receive. In moments of weakness, grab the list and give yourself a dose of positive thinking.

Lighten up on yourself. This is no big deal. So what if you found a bad habit in your repertoire of behaviors? Isn't it great that you've found it, and can now transform it? Aren't you glad you didn't have to live with it for another five years? Aren't you excited about revealing and transforming yet another layer of distorted beliefs that have been clogging up your happiness? Doesn't it feel great each time you catch yourself in an old pattern because you know that each discovery brings you closer to revealing and expressing your fullness?

25

Summoning Financial Freedom

(by Tom Haskins)

Each of us have enjoyed "making more money than ever before." For many, our first experience was getting an allowance that enabled us to buy things without parental involvement. You may have gone from the sporadic cash flow of baby-sitting to the steady income of part-time work after school. In jobs, we experienced how good it feels to get raises, bonuses, and promotions. You may have felt the freedom of making more money by changing employment, starting a small business, or getting more schooling which generated new job offers. Some of us have also enjoyed investing capital and receiving dividends, rental income or interest payments.

Each of these experiences gives us a glimpse at how good it feels to "manifest abundance." We can afford more extravagant purchases. We learn what it's like to be free from financial limitations and our own past histories. We think about ways to earn more money because it feels good. All these experiences I have just described are "third dimensional." They provide financial freedom— at a cost. They offer short-lived pleasures. They are freedoms which can be taken away by downsizing, pay cuts, budget tightening, economic inflation, or downturns in money markets. The freedom can be lost by simply finding how much money other people are being paid or are charging for their services. The feeling of freedom also vanishes as we spend more than we earn and look forward to our next increase.

There is no real freedom in "making more money than before." It's not the kind of freedom our Higher Selves have in mind for us to enjoy. Those flirtations with abundance whet our appetite for "simply asking the Universe for what we want." It awakens the hunger for a kind of freedom that cannot be taken away. The frustrations of passing pleasures get us asking better questions and seeking metaphysical answers. Once the longing for lasting freedom is awakened, channeled wisdom like the following from Chief Joseph resonates with us.

"You no longer need to "earn" your living or your way through life. You don't need to "earn" anything. It is your birthright; abundance in every form is your birthright as a child of the Great Spirit, of the Universe. You don't need to earn it—it's already yours. All you NEED to do is to command it to manifest. It's that simple." (Sentinels of the Sky Issue #15 *GreatWesternPublishing*)

At this point, we want to manifest miracles and are blocked from receiving them. We are disconnected from continual inspiration and we long for reconnection. We ask the Universe for what we want and get disappointed by "no shows" and "more of what we did not want." We feel trapped in our persistent unwanted circumstances, and foiled when we try to find a way out.

The problem of being stuck like this can be pictured as "having fresh ideas in our head and leftovers in our heart." The tone we broadcast from our hearts is not current with our highly evolved desires. We are signaling the Universe for more "heartfelt" financial limitations, while thinking we want to summon financial freedom.

Our Higher Selves get us to "clean out the leftovers in our hearts" with fantasies of windfall amounts of cash. They fill our minds with awesome scenarios of wealth and financial freedom. The purpose of every lottery and sweepstakes ticket that is purchased is to get people imagining the unlimited financial freedom their Higher Selves have in mind. The inundation of our imagination with tantalizing spending levels uplifts the leftover tone of our heart from the all-too-familiar vibes of self pity, lack and limitation. We gain experiences of FEELING free of financial limitations which counteract the MEMORIES of financial limitations and losses.

Each leftover memory of financial hardship became a rigid belief which blocks the freedom we seek to summon. At the time, we sought protection from being victimized by our own naivete, wishful thinking or gullibility. We thought we got an upper hand by realizing "what the facts are," yet we "locked ourselves into lack" by making up our minds about how to avoid a repeat of what we did not want to experience. We dedicate our "pursuit of happiness" to an endless loop of those unwanted experiences. This is called "karma," "clinging to illusions," "living in the past" or "asking for trouble." It's the opposite of forgiving, letting go, going with the flow and unconditional love.

A way out of this endless loop becomes obvious when we face the leftover feelings in our hearts. We see how we have been acting impossible to please. We stop complaining about the program on the TV when we realize we put the tape in the VCR. We see how we've been simply fussing at the perfect match to how fussy we are in our hearts. When we get the picture of how we "do this to ourselves," we instantly have the power to "do" what we want to ourselves instead. We see how perfect all these unwanted experiences look to our Higher Selves.

We stop thinking that we know what we want. We ask, "What do I want?" and RECEIVE delightful answers from our Higher Selves. We realize we have to RELEASE the blockages from past experiences. We then RESONATE in our hearts with the feelings that match the desires we received from our Higher Selves. Our imaginations are filled with images that give us the feeling of already having what we now know we really want. We are summoning what we meant to receive. (For more on the three R's, see: Creating your Own Reality II-Sentinels of the Sky Issue #4)

It may continue to look to other people that we are earning money. However, it won't feel like that to us. We will be basking in the experience of receiving what we want, summoning what is ours to experience, living the connection to our Higher Selves. It will seem like we are frolicking in a kind of freedom that cannot be taken away from us. We will be doing what we want to because it feels good, not "doing what we have to do" because of the "facts of life about earning money."

It won't matter how this looks to other people. Our life will revolve around the feelings we choose to resonate in our hearts, which are best kept free of what other people think. We will radiate with the joy of fulfilling our unique destiny by summoning our financial freedom. We will feel in our hearts what we want to broadcast to our surroundings. We will then experience reflections of those feelings as life dances before us at the nonstop wedding of our Higher Selves and human lives.

You can find Tom's Biography on the Biography page.

26

17–34–68 Second Corner—Tools for Creating!

(by Susan James)

There are two "skills" that I have developed as habit that have made a HUGE difference in my days. My days are incredible!

1) I have a habit of stating out loud how I desire things to be. I make these statements as though I already had the "thing" or "situation" in my present experience.

2) I have my own system of how I visualize my desires; one was mentioned in my previous essay.

Please do not underestimate the effect of using these tools in your life to bring you the life that you desire!

Affirmation & Visualizing and Daydreaming

27

How I Manifested a Subdivision

(by Susan James)

Several years ago, my profession was one of Pharmaceutical Sales. At that time I knew I did not want to "be" that forever, and I set about creating more money flow somehow. I was led to study, and yes, I did study—"No Money Down" Real Estate. This simply fit into what I was wanting for my overall life, and it fit into my present, at that time.

My study usually involved the housing market, but what I was getting good at was structuring "the deal." You see, the cool part about Real Estate that I learned is that there are no rules. You can make it up anyway you want. It's your game, and your deal! (Just like Life, once you "get it!")

I stayed excited about all of this! I had M.L.S. books, I had my favorite Real Estate Agent, who of course loved no money down deals—(not!), I played with numbers, I had the little book that tells you what the payments are, including interest for all ratios you could imagine. This was a fun game for me, just learning and being excited about pulling this off, somehow. Now a key here, since this is about how to manifest what you want, is that I never thought about it NOT happening. I didn't push, I just played, and I knew and expected to have this work out; I was not concerned about how, and when and where and who!

THEN ONE DAY a friend of mine, also in the same work field, and I made plans to meet for lunch. She knew, due to previous conversations, that I was studying the No money down real estate stuff, but I would just mention it in passing, as some folks get bored with all the excitement of others!

ANYWAY, we are in the car. I am driving, and she says, "Susan, I know you've been studying the real estate stuff and I've got a chunk of money. I do not have the interest in the study of what you are doing, but I do have an interest in putting my money to work, and I know you can pull this off!" She then went on to say, that she had inquired about a subdivision, and "would this be something you would be interested in being a partner with me in?"

Now, you have got to know, that as the words were rolling out of her mouth, they were coming at me in slow motion...! I am driving and thinking...'Wow, this is it, this is the "deal" of the century! My "no money down" real estate deal was manifesting before my eyes in that moment! This was O.P.M., (other peoples money), I needed no upstart capital! Dream done!'

So the general agreement came down to this: she had the dollars, and I agreed to structure the deal. The owner of the property was willing to "owner finance," so the rest was made in "heaven," because that's what I knew how to do! So the deal was done between me and my friend. It just so happened that about 30 days later there was a huge Medical meeting in New Orleans which both of us were attending, and during this meeting we tied up the loose ends. What a great city to tie up loose ends of a perfect deal! New Orleans is one of my favorite cities, as I have been there five times. So it was perfect. But now to the Manifest part. What made this work out?

One: I chose what I wanted to happen.

Two: I intended for it to happen, without placing any restrictions on how and when it came.

Three: I stayed in the excited and expectant mode. I believed I would pull this off; I just did not know how, and I did not think about HOW!

Four: I never thought about it NOT coming.

So how did it come? Through a friend that I knew and trusted, and this friend knew and trusted me. It came bigger and better in the fact that this was a subdivision, and not a house. I mean how exciting was that, that I pulled that one off?

The point that I hope that you get, is that you have so much Love/Energy/God/Universe, whatever you wish to call it, at your disposal! It is there for you to put to "work" and you can "trust this." It moves mountains for you. All you have to do is choose what you want, intend for it to happen, expect for it to happen, be excited that you know it is happening, and the events, the circumstances, the people, the situations, just unfold like magic before your very eyes!

This is how life is supposed to be for all of us! We have been "taught" by well-meaning folks BACKWARDS. Life is so much easier and more fun and more abundant when you cross that line of "Oh, I get it now!"

So Dream, and Dream Big, and get excited about it actually appearing in your life, and watch for signs and signals that it is coming. The Big ole' Universe sends you symbols and signs that what you say and what you choose is on its way. But if you change your mind, if you think it won't come, the Universe loves you enough to bring you that also. It simply gives you what you think about; that's the only guideline we have. So think on purpose, choose on purpose, intend on purpose, stop MUCKING with your life. It is supposed to be fun and wonderful! (And yes, mine is, thank you very, very much!)

My love to you!
Susan

28

17–34–68 Second Corner—Tools for Creating!

(by Susan James)

"You have been given an active imagination; it is your doorway out of where you are." (Sonya Roman, "Living in Joy")

AND SO, what are some ways to use your imagination to create what you want? WRITE, WRITE, WRITE, AFFIRM, AFFIRM, AFFIRM, DAYDREAM, DAYDREAM, DAYDREAM!

(ALL in the "first person!" I AM, I have, It is!)

29

What Is a Manifestation, Anyway?

(by Susan James)

Just what is a "manifestation," anyway, and how do I really know that what I want is mine?

1. It's already here. I just need to know how to get to it. I already know what "it's already here" really means.

2. There is this "box" and there is this lid on this box.

3. When this box of mine is "full" of one "manifestation" on top of another, and another, and another, then my box will be full and my end result is that my "overall" intention just shows up.

4. Which means, every time I have a "good feeling" about what I want, that "good feeling" in and of itself is a "manifestation"; it is a "real" thing. It goes in the box automatically. Every time I think a good thought, it goes in the box. Even when I have a good thought about something not related to my desire, it is still a "manifestation thing," and it goes in the box, automatically.

5. The box begins to fill up.

6. Every time I notice what I notice, and it is a good thing, it goes in the box.

7. Every time I see a "signal" or sign" or "symbol" that relates to my desire in some way, and I also give recognition that it is a communication from the Universe; those things, too, are "manifestations," and they go in the

box, The box is filling nicely and that feels good, too, and even that goes in the box.

8. I see a license plate that I know is meant for me...It goes in the box.

9. I see a billboard that I know is meant for me...It goes in the box.

10. I hear a song that I know is meant for me...It goes in the box.

11. I overhear a conversation and the only phrase that I hear I know is "meant" for me...It goes in the box.

12. The more I believe and trust in the stuff going in the box, the faster I get more stuff to put in the box, and the faster the box fills, and the faster my box fills, the quicker I get my ultimate desire, and it is even better than I thought it would be.

13. But if I start to question the things in the box, If I stay in those doubtful, fearful, lackful places too long, some of the stuff starts leaving the box, one by one, and then the box begins to empty.

14. But the cool thing about the Universe is that I get to put stuff back in the box whenever I want to, and I can fill it up as fast as I think I can, and want to and intend to.

15. YOU do know how to fill up YOUR box, don't you? Good, I thought you did, and I get to put that nice confidence that I have in you IN MY Box!

16. And what is in Susan's Box? Well just for starters, I have lots of license plates, lots of billboards, lots of songs, lots of overheard conversations, lots of newspaper and magazine headlines, lots of words from unknowing friends, lots of smiles, lots of looking at mens butts...(did you really read this far?), lots of "knowing" that this all works, lots of the Universe and My higher self giving me stuff out of nowhere.

My Box is full, and you know what is next...

Love Susan

31

Making the Decision to Feel Good

(by Susan James)

One of my turning points, meaning my knowledge-turned-into-experience, was when Jeff Forte in his original newsletter kept banging away at this phrase: *"I have made the decision that nothing is more important than that I feel good, which draws like a magnet all good things to me."*

What is so important about "feeling good" in this manifesting thing, this "creating on purpose" thing? The Universe does not hear your words. It hears your "vibration." Your vibration is another term for "emotions/feelings." You know you have heard "you can't fool Mother Nature"; this applies here. If you say one thing but "feel" another, the Universe delivers to you based on your "feelings."

So the "work" is in changing your "feelings/emotion/vibration" to one of a higher energy. You do this by feeling good.

Feeling good—about what? Anything that takes your mind off what does not make you feel good. The reason that it is so important for us to grasp this is that when you have emotions of just plain feeling good for more and more of your day, this puts you in the place of the Universe "matching" your vibration with the things that you already told it that make you feel good. You have been telling the Universe for years what makes you feel good.

You have done it through desire, you have done it in your wishing and hoping. But alas, also in those past years, you mixed the bag with stuff that did not make you feel so good. You canceled out much of the good stuff that was on its way to you. *Even Steven*, so to speak—or *Stuck in the Muck*.

So, the point here is begin to "pay attention" in your day. Is what you just heard from someone, what you just said to someone, what you were just thinking about. Did it feel good, or did it not feel good?

If it did not feel good, change it—quickly. If it did not feel good, then you are moving away from all the things that you say you want. Is it that easy? Yes, and that is the point.

You do not have to feel good about the thing that you want or the thing that is making you feel not good; you just have to feel good about ANYTHING! It is never about the "subject," it is always about the "vibration."

To end this, as you "think" on these things you will realize how expensive it is for your life to "not feel good," and you will reach the point in your "knowing" that no matter what, you will make the decision that nothing is more important than that you feel good.

My Best to You...Susan
P.S. Did I mention "feel good" enough times?...

32

Deciding What Is Truth

(by Carol James)

From the infinite ream of "truths," each of us decides which truths to believe, just as we decide the meanings we make about our situations and experiences. Using beliefs as a foundation, we move forward creating our life through our thoughts, choices and actions. If we like the results we get while embodying the truths we've embraced, we can assume that those truths are working for us. If we don't like the results we get, we have several choices. We can…

> Keep the truths that do not work, and spend our time complaining about them.
> Keep the truths that do not work, and find a way to make them work.
> Keep the truths that do not work, and blame our undesirable results on those who taught us those truths.
> Seek to find which truths do not serve us, and find out why.
> Seek to find which truths do not serve us, and transform them into something more aligned with beliefs that do work.
> Let go of the truths that don't serve us.
> In this world of abundant truths from which to choose, isn't it great that we have the free will to choose which ones to pick and which ones to ignore?

33

On Letting Go...

(by Susan James)

When we let go of wondering if it's gonna turn out all right, and just know that it is—it always does.

When we let go of wondering where it's gonna come from, and just know that it is coming—it always does.

When we let go of thoughts containing "adverse situations'" and replace them with our dreams and the stuff that we want, we begin to feel better.

When most of our thoughts throughout the day are about what we want to happen, and if ever they occasionally take us to what we don't want to happen, we know how to fix it. We change what we are thinking about. It is mental Judo.

HOWEVER, in this mental Judo, it is the only discipline we need. We can do that. The rewards of thinking only about what we want are worth the new habits that we had to form.

Our thoughts create our future, and we know exactly what that means. We do know exactly what that means. Our thoughts create our future, that is what that means.

Susan

34

The Difference Between "Needing" & "Wanting"

(by Susan James)

There is no difference between the "thing" and the "form." It is all about the experience and the feeling reaction.

This is what I have found out and experienced:

As long as I "feel good," the stuff that I want shows up.

If I "need" it, it takes a long time in coming, if at all.

Once you get to the point that you honestly "believe" that the most important thing you can do is to "feel good," then all the stuff that you want (not need) begins to show up.

If it is a complex matter, the Universe sends you manifestations that the big thing that you want is coming, trust those signs; they add to your feeling good and the believability that it is indeed coming, which again makes you feel good if you believe it!

Here is where I am:

I am so very clear on what I want.

I have not defined "how" I want it to come to me.

I have defined what I want, and why I want it.

The reason we want anything is because it makes us feel good! That is the only reason we flow energy towards what we want—so that we feel good!

Once you have told the Universe what you want and why you want it, then the very next step is to do whatever it takes to make you feel good. You can think about or do anything to make yourself feel good; it does not have to be related to what you want. The Universe heard you the first time. Your only job is to keep your vibrational tone (feelings) in a happy good place, no matter what!

There is a difference between "needing" something and "wanting/intending/ desiring." Once you know "that" difference, it all gets more and more clear. The law of attraction keeps it from you if you "need" it. It brings it to you if you "want" it!

Figure it out; you can, and you know it!

Love Susan

35

What Does Love Have to Do with Money?

(by Susan James)

Every once in a while, while writing these articles, I just have to get "right down to it," and this is another of those times. So just get ready.

We all lead an existence that requires money to make our worlds go round, not only for the present needs going on, but for the future desires.

Now we all have a choice. We can suffocate ourselves in concern of where is it going to come from and will we ever be able to do what we really "want?" OR, we can just know that it will just show up! (It does, you know)

So let me tell you the Truth as I have experienced it. The more often in a day that I am happy and feeling good, all of the "stuff" that is required to make my world comfortable and fun just shows up. That is a fact. (And I feel good 98% of my day, so you have to know that my life is pretty incredible.)

It not only is Fact, it is Universal/God Law. That is why it works. PERIOD.

"The most important thing you can do in each and every moment is to feel good." PERIOD.

And why? There is this "stream," and when you are standing in this stream everything that you consider to be good in and for your life Just Shows Up! It is LAW!

When you step out of that stream, you then are not in benefit of the good things coming up. They just float right by and you do not even see them. When you ARE in the stream, you also miss many negative things that may have come your way. This stream works both ways for you, depending on if you are in or out of it.

So what does Love have to do with Money? Love is Energy. Period. Energy is in and around everything. Which means, Love is Energy. This also means that Love is Money, and Money is Love. Those wonderful green dollar bills and other colors of those of other countries reading this, it is all just made up of energy—of little molecules of big Love.

That's all it is. Because Money and Dollars help all of us "live" in this world, as we pass it from hand to hand, for service to service, we are simply just passing Love around. It is just "God's Love Paper"—that is all Money is!

So how do you get more of "God's Love Paper" to show up in your life?

Step #one:	You ASK!
Step #two:	Feel as good as you can in every moment of the day. (Stream)

That's it, Babe. It is that simple. It has always been this simple. WE HAVE BEEN TAUGHT BACKWARDS! DO YOU GET THIS?

Since I am now yelling...<grin>. I will take it one step further. Because I know many of you are asking, "Great, Susan, BUT how do I feel good about all of this stuff that is not right in my life so I can stay in that Stream?".

Answer: You do not look at that stuff. You tell the Universe what you desire and need, and you do so by being thankful that it has shown up in someway, and you have not tried to manage the results. You intend. You make decisions that you will be not be denied the happiness and joy and abundance that is your birthright. YOU DID NOT COME HERE TO LIVE IN LIMITATION. YOU NEED TO KNOW THAT!

God & The Universe is so Loving and abundant, and they want us to have it all. We just forgot that. It is now time to remember!

And you begin by remembering this, by choosing more things in your day that you really want to do, and stop doing those things that you think you "should" do. You first must take care of yourselves and your own love for yourself before you can spread it to others. Yes, you need to be selfish, and most importantly you need to "unlearn" that selfish is a "bad" thing! It is not; it is most beautiful, as you all are!

I am done. I intend for much bounty and wisdom and fun for all eyes reading these words.

My Love to You!
Susan

36

Seek and You Shall Find

(by Susan James)

"Seek and You Shall Find"

> **Question:** What do you Seek now?
> **Answer:** (you fill in the blank)

How do you find it? By Seeking it.

How do you seek it? (Other words for seek: ASK and request) Ask and you will find. What are you asking for? Which means…? Simply because I ASK, I FIND. Therein lies your power, in your knowing of this.

Simple: It is a true statement that "simply" because you ask, it is. Period. RELAX in this knowing.

37

How Do You Enter the Door of Abundance?

(by Susan James)

Question:	HOW DO YOU ENTER THE DOOR OF ABUNDANCE?
Answer:	*YOU PUSH ON IT WITH YOUR INTENT!*

And so, what does this mean? What is an intention? It is a "decision." There is power in decision. You make a decision; you have then placed an intention out to the Universe/God. It is in that intent and that decision that the door of Abundance opens to you.

It is when you do not make intentions about your life that you end up reacting to things and people, instead of controlling them. By controlling them— meaning that if you had placed an intention around an issue and did not allow fear to change your mind—the situations begin to mold more towards your liking. WHY? Well, it is LAW!

So whatever you are on the fence about—DECIDE! And about tomorrow— decide how it will be for you. State Your Claim! And then Follow Your Heart!

Oh, and by the way, in case you do not yet know this: The Ultimate Goal: is to "release all fear, and know only unlimitedness."

38

Trust…But Can You Really Trust It?

(by Susan James)

I know about this trust thing; just ask me. I have thrown caution to the wind—wished upon a star—hoped for the best—gone out on a limb, and jumped without a net!

And I know some of you whose eyes grace these words have done the same thing. Where is your brain? What do you mean, you have no other plan, other than trust? Trust in what? The wind? The Unknown…?

Trust in Spirit? You say, "Are you Crazy?" "Are you insane?" Do you know how close insanity and genius are?

Does any of this sound or feel familiar? And where has it gotten me? Here is where it has gotten "me."

1. My skin and the "All that Is" is the same. I am that close. The "All that Is" speaks to me, and I not only know it; I feel it! Do you even have any idea what that means? I think a thought, and Spirit in that moment tells me "stuff." I am given "visions…"

   Now for a while when I began this "stuff," I did not know the difference between what a vision was and my daydreaming or visualizing. But NOW I know, because I am sent visions. And is this cool or what? It's not something I have to wonder—"Did I make that up?" (not that it matters, cause making it up is a good thing), but visions are "things" that just show up. Before the "visions" came the "blocks of thought"—out of "nowhere!"

AND, when I make this statement—"I am connected to Divine Flow"—my heart jumps! And I feel love all over the place...

2. And you know...I have been in this Joy place for a good while, and good stuff just happens to me, but NOW it is this BLISS place. Joy is grand, but Bliss, well, that is sweeter-, and you "feel" the difference!

3. But lets get back to the Manifesting stuff...That's why we are all here, anyway. Can you pay the rent with this stuff? Will your dreams come true? Can you feed your families? And heck, can you have FUN? Don't you just want to have fun sometimes? Just freedom and Fun?

4. The answer is this: yes. I practice what I say here. I have no fear or anxiety about money not showing up; it just shows up. Have all of my dreams and desires manifested in my "now," so that I may touch them? Nope, not all of them—yet. But they Are. How do I know? Because the "All that Is"—God, Spirit, my soul, my higher self, they all confirm it for me. Do I trust "THEM"? Do I trust "THAT?" GOD, YES! THERE IS NO OTHER WAY!

Susan

39

Molding Energy & Using Your Inner Being/Higher Self

(by Susan James)

1. "You are not molding clay in this environment; you are molding energy. You mold energy by thinking thoughts ' by thinking and feeling, thinking and feeling, thinking and feeling"

2. "Trust the way you feel. If you feel crummy (disappointment, anger, hurt frustration, negative), YOU ARE NOT connected to allowing what you want."

3. "You could convince yourself of three very important things"

   A. Your Inner Being/Higher Self Exists

   B. Your Inner Being/Higher Self is Pure Positive Energy

   C. You have instant, ready, constant, always access to that connection of pure positive energy.

4. "Negative feelings, you are vibrationally disallowing your connection to your own inner being."

"In other words, you literally have access to the Infinite Intelligence as far as you are able to allow it to come through."

Love Susan
(Resource: Abraham-Hicks Publications: http://www.abraham-hicks.com)

40

Manifestation of Our Farm

(by B. W.)

This is but one of many manifesting stories that I have personally had the pleasure of experiencing in my life. It always such fun when dreams do come true! Before I begin, I would like to tell you that being a small business owner, we had heard that it is almost impossible to get financing unless you have cash in the bank to back it up. COLLATERAL. We did not! We had the equity in our house, and lots of other things that banks don't like to use for collateral. Our income was good, but we did not have collateral on paper: the stuff banks love. So here we go. Let the dreams begin!

My husband and I had been looking and looking for a new house so we could combine our business and our home on one property, thence paying one mortgage, instead of two checks a month totaling $2,400.00 per month. For a year we searched. We had piles of information on building houses, shops for the business, land, blueprints, price lists, listings from Realtors, Master plans, building requirements—in fact we had everything in order, and we narrowed down exactly what we wanted.

We looked and looked. We looked at every house on the market for miles and miles. We knew exactly what we wanted: location, price, land, etc. Although we did not have that specific house yet in physical sight, we were so clear on exactly what we needed and wanted.

In the mean time, we had two floods in our home. #1 the hoses from the washing machine burst during the night and left 2 feet of water in the rec. room. Hence the insurance company redecorated our entire Family Room with new walls, ceilings and carpet. #2 flood one week later: the water line for the toilet broke, and consequently the insurance company replaced the remaining carpets in the house. All this for a $500.00 deductible. Previously, our company built a new flagstone patio and walkway in the back, along with beautiful plantings and a pond with a waterfall. We were almost ready to sell.

A couple of months later, in July, we finished preparing our house for sale. We invested another $500.00 or so for an extensive cleaning and patching up a few things and put a new floor in the front hall. We looked at EVERY single house in our neighborhood that was for sale. We knew exactly what our competition was. So now it was August, and we took the plunge. Our friend who lived in our neighborhood was our realtor. He said we should be prepared to wait at least a year to sell. That's how long the typical house in this neighborhood is on the market. He also told us that we should not ask too high a price. I said "NOPE. THIS HOUSE WILL SELL IN 1 MONTH!" He just laughed. I laughed back and I said "WE WILL SEE—just watch!" I was very confident, and never had the thought that it would not be exactly as I chose.

During this time, we placed a contract on a piece of land not far from us that had 25 acres. We loved this piece of land. Although I was a little hesitant, for we would have to build everything here (house, barn, shop, fencing, etc.) and it did not have a source of natural water, which was on my list. But we bid anyway and thought we could make it work. They were asking $235,000.00 for the land, and we knew that was too much, so we offered $145,000.00. The realtor said that was way too low. We said, "Well, we won't lose anything here; let's see what happens." We placed a deposit with the signed contract, and let it fly. They came back almost immediately. "NO WAY, but how about $195,000.00?" We said, "OK. then how about $155,000.00?" "NO WAY, but how about $175,000.00?" We said "How about $165,000.00?" They said "NO WAY, NO HOW!" And so we left and said, "Call us if you change your minds." Nothing lost! We found that we loved playing this game! Now remember, this place for it pops up again.

Then came fall. The last house we looked at was in another county—just over the border of where we were looking. We drove up to the driveway, saw the sign and called the home that we were looking at. The woman answered and told us that they had just taken this house off the market. They did not want to sell. Darn! This place looked like it had real potential! So we left and got on to other business.

We got busy with our jobs and work and placed our search on hold for the time being. Although we never gave up on our dream; our dreams still lived within us! We went over the budget once again and realized that WE STILL NEEDED ANOTHER $50K to make this work.

Well, four weeks went by—No sale, and my realtor said, "See? I told you so!" I said, "It's not over until the fat lady sings!" The next week, the house sold! 5 WEEKS! (Some months have five weeks) AND it sold for $2K more than we were asking! GO FIGURE. Now we had to find a rental until winter was over and we found another house to buy. I went to work. I found a house in our neighborhood. My intentions were $1,000 a month and the same bus and the same school for kids. PETS ALLOWED. MONTH TO MONTH BASIS, because if we found something we had to move on it quickly.

I FOUND IT! It was in the same neighborhood as our old house. The owners got transferred and had to move ASAP. Their house did not sell, so I just asked them. The woman said that she wanted $1,200 a month and I said $1,000. She said that she did not like that, but OK. Then I said I have pets. She said she did NOT like that, but OK. I said I need a month-to-month rental and she said "URGGG, but OK."

So we moved down the street. Winter came and I was thinking, I just put all this money from the sale of my house in my bank account and was really focused on having loads! WINTER CAME, 95/96 SNOW STORM OF THE CENTURY CAME! Yes, we plow snow and we made exactly $50K—exactly what we needed to buy our dream.

We called our realtor and said we were ready. Spring was coming, and our busiest season was about to begin. FAST! We need this FAST! At this point, we both did not even care what the house looked like. We joked and said, "Just give us a trailer with a good roof and plumbing, and we're in business!" We just wanted to MOVE, and we were READY!

Our realtor gave us a printout. We drove to the first house. We looked and looked at it from the road. I said, "Hey! We were here in the FALL, looking from the road, and we wanted to look at this house in the Fall (before we had the $50K), and when we called from the car phone they said that they just took it off the market. THEY WERE NOT SELLING. So now it was February, after that huge snow storm. The house was on the market again—FOR $100,000 LESS THAN IN THE FALL! RIGHT IN OUR BALL PARK.

We drove into the driveway (very long driveway and we were just at the bottom); we saw the complete shop (for the business)—PERFECT!—we saw the fencing for the horses we had always wanted—PERFECT! We saw the wonderful creek that we always wanted—PERFECT! We saw the hay barns, the woods, the 24 acres (we wanted between 10 and 25 acres) and everything just seemed PER-FECT, and we did not even look at the house or walk the property; we just sat at the end of the driveway and both in unison said "IT'S OURS."

Then we saw the house. OH, MY GOD! IT WAS GORGEOUS! Beautiful wide plank wooden floors, modern conveniences, EVERYTHING, including a spare bedroom. PERFECTO! We signed the papers, being self-employed and having a brother-in-law as our banker, we did not have to give out any information on salaries—which was good, because that just would have caused major disruption. BUT WE KNEW IT WOULD WORK! IT HAD TO!

The woman did not want to sell, but they had to because her husband was sick and not able to make any money. She kept telling me that we would not qualify and that this would not work. I just kept smiling and saying that it was all fine! We offered them $28K less than the asking price, and the realtor said "That's too low." I said "NOPE, it's perfect, and we will get it." We bought for what we offered! AND the mortgage was $2,400.00—exactly what we intended!

WE MOVED IN MARCH of 1996, and it's all history from there! We actually walked the property after we moved in, and found that each day we found something else that was on our list and it was HERE! WE HAD IT ALL! We even bought equipment from the guy that we needed now that we had a farm. He had it all in the SHOP and for a GOOD PRICE! AND WE HAD THE MONEY IN OUR POCKETS!

And so, that is the story of OUR FARM!

Oh, and remember that piece of land that we bid on? Well, they called one month after we moved into our farm. They said, "Remember that $165,000.00 you bid? Well it's yours." I said, "A day late and a dollar short!"

SUMMARY:

1) We had a Thought.

2) Which turned into a DESIRE.

3) We pondered, mused, studied about, dreamed, envisioned, imagined our desire until it felt real and alive. We lived our DESIRE in every thought we had about our desire.

4) We kept our thoughts ONLY on what we chose for our desire, and if we wandered we pulled back and said, "No—THIS IS WHAT WE

CHOOSE!" We did NOT listen to others who said it was not possible or anything negative about it!

5) We made it fun, and we allowed it in our lives!

6) We had no other choices but OUR DESIRE!

7) IT MANIFESTED in our life. It was already real in our dreams, and it manifested when we allowed it! It manifested in our physical lives, because it had no other choice BUT TO!

B. W.

41

Write Before You Call!

(by Susan James)

I had a phone call to make that I was feeling uncomfortable about. I have taught myself not be uncomfortable for long; it's too expensive.

So right before the phone call, I wrote down:

> *Relax, this is easy*
> *Ease*
> *Ease*
>
> *I intend for this phone call to go smoothly. The conditions will all work out easily in my favor. I have this completely under my control, simply because I know more. So help me with this, Spirit; help me be calm and matter-of-fact about this.*

While I was "in" the phone call, I was continuing to write: *This is easy. I am at peace. This is not serious. It is going well. This is no big deal.*

Result: The entire phone call went absolutely great and it ALL worked out in my favor.

You can apply this to ANY situation: Relationship/Financial Issues. If it is important to you, then grab the pen and paper and rule your world!

Comment: You have control; just take it!

Love Susan

42

Why Go to All the Trouble? Maybe It's All a Joke!

(by Susan James)

Why go to the trouble...to read things like this? What if it really does not work? What if there is cosmic joke somewhere, and we have been duped, me included? How can you measure, as you go along? Well, let's use my life as the test:

1. I laugh a whole lot.

2. I love a whole lot.

3. I am loved a whole lot.

4. I hardly ever, never, am in a "bad mood."

5. Seldom is there any problem or challenge in my life.

6. If a challenge does show up, I write it on a piece of paper,and *poof* it works out.

7. I stay slim; food is no problem. I eat as much and whatever I choose.

8. I am in excellent health.

9. I have no fear or worries about money issues.

10. I have no fears or anxieties about relationship issues.

11. I am standing in this incredible place of being able to just watch my life come to me.

12. I live my days as a happy millionaire would. I am free to do whatever I choose.

13. My work/livelihood is incredibly fun and fulfilling.

Seems to me, this "stuff" works! I vote YES! It all does work. What is different about my life versus before? Well before, I was still an optimistic, positive person—enthusiastic—but I had "stuff" within all of that...and around that...always having to work through or knock down something or go through something.

Realizing that was a good place to be was not enough for a really wonderful, incredible life. So I kept looking and asking—and the "tools" of "creating on purpose " the life I desired, found their way into my life. So, yeah, that's why you and I read this kind of material; it "works." But, YOU have to do the "work." (i.e., apply/use the tools, develop the skills of manifesting your desires)

So keep going, keep reading till you are sick of it; then you will have it in your blood, and you will never look back, because the future is so darn incredible— and paved with this wonderful present. And the past does not exist, except to remind you how far you have come.

As Always,
Susan

43

Manifesting Your Desires

(by John Welsh)

A couple of things happened to me just a few months ago. Things were unwinding and falling apart. My planned creations were not making it into form, or when they did, it was not what I wanted. Things were just not in sync.

What I realized is that I wanted the essence of what these things could give me, but the specific forms that came along I just took, even though they were only partially satisfying. For me it was a lesson in discernment about things that match who I am. My little projects that didn't happen really weren't totally in alignment with who I know myself to be at this point in my life. They reflected an old me, and a confused me. Sort of like it was forms from the past manifesting too late in the future because I sort of fell out of the flow. Falling out of the flow, in my opinion, comes from getting lazy and complacent with what our life is about. Also, I think lack of inspiration has a lot to do with it.

Insufficient vision into one's higher path, or even the lack of energy to create a fantastic life. Luckily, though, being 24, my impatience gets the best of me, so when I fall out of the flow and I realize that I'm not getting what I know I deserve and can have, that little voice inside starts giving me a million reasons to sit down and start working on my reality creating with renewed interest. "You want that car, don't you? You want that house, don't you? Hey, don't forget about that Prada suit you saw!"

Another thing that I learned was that things like these can be followed by confusion, which is a very high state of mind! The mind is opening to new thoughts and realities, and doesn't have a grip on the old, and the new hasn't really solidified. The in-between state. That's where it's time to make some choices and really call on your higher power to assist you. Allow the Universe to step in a bit and guide where your ground crew (your conscious mind, emotions and body) are going. So I said, "Forget it." Let it all go and lots of new things will come in shortly thereafter. I shed my skin, so to speak. Once I realized what was happening, it became a lot more fun, and I felt a lot more free. I think in these cases self-observation is an important tool. By making it a habit, you become the captain of your own ship, and when you need guidance, you've let go of just enough of your ego to realize that there is definitely a bigger picture.

Speaking of the bigger picture, I also learned something else about my desires and the Higher Will of the Universe. No matter what, they are the same! You can want all the money you can get your hands on, be as materialistic as you want, but when you allow yourself to accept those things as Divine in themselves, then those desires and worldly possessions become instrumental in helping make that Higher Will a reality in your life! Life is supposed to be fun and exciting. If having "things" makes it more fun for you, then it's already been approved by your Higher Self (which approves everything by the way, and can't really do anything "wrong," just different paths to the same end). Don't forget, your Higher Self is all about creating and making things happen. It's just a matter of allowing yourself to have those things. I think that the Universe is always trying to give us what we want, but it's only ourselves that get in the way of that form of Divine Intervention.

Working on cleaning house in your mind is a good way to start opening to the new life you are in the midst of creating. If you haven't manifested everything that you want by now, then you've still got some work to do. I tried to fool myself for a long time, but after a while it became pretty apparent that I had to make some changes in how I felt about many different things, even things that seemed unrelated. Once I did start getting hard core about it, then it was like the Universe said, "YES, YES, YES" and BOOM! Doors open, things come and even more of my path has been revealed to me. It's really exciting when this happens! I love it!

Fear not, keep your mind on what you do want to experience, in essence, like love, prosperity, happiness, and those things will come! Just be willing to grow, and keep your mind focused on your growth instead of getting all wrapped up in the forms that you want your growth to take. Eventually, they will both be one. This is totally true. I'm getting to that point, and it's just getting better every day!

John Welsh

44

Trusting Your Impulses

(by Kristen Fox)

Some of the most common questions about inner guidance usually sound something like this: "Can we REALLY let go and simply trust our spontaneity and inner guidance? Won't everything fall apart if we don't monitor and control all the details in our lives? And why is this 'simple' step so difficult?"

Many times when we have to put overt effort into maintaining some sort of life style or level of appearance, it is as if we're trying to run away from feeling or experiencing our fears or beliefs. For instance, perhaps you are in a relationship with an extremely tidy person and you are not especially tidy yourself. Because you fear your partner will judge you or leave you because of your habits, you put a lot of energy into maintaining a facade of tidiness, despite your more casual leanings.

This is often why some people stay in jobs they don't like, although since the belief that you have to "earn a living" is so common in our culture, we often see it as "just the way things are." The belief that we aren't innately supported by the Universe, coupled with the belief in separation from the Source, brings up feelings of fear and lack.

What does this have to do with being spontaneous and trusting our impulses? When we decide that we can no longer work at maintaining a situation that holds no joy for us, such as the job we hate or the facade of being someone we're not, one of the first things that happens is that we come face-to-face with FEAR. Intuitively, we know this will happen when we cease our effortful behavior, when we allow the walls we've built inside to crumble. Once the walls start to dissolve, our unfelt emotions of fear are RIGHT THERE. The fears tell us that we must do or be something extra in order to have what we want—that we must clean our house every day in order to keep our partner or work that job in order to pay the bills. The fear FEELS quite real.

On the other hand, our impulses will tell us to quit that job or let go and trust and leave the dirty dishes in the sink for a day, and all we will lose is the illusion of placing our trust and the power of creation outside our reach. This is where we have to summon our courage in order to bring that trust and easefulness into practice in our reality.

Here's a simple example that illustrates taking at least a tiny leap of faith despite the fears involved. Quite a few years ago, when I was still a full-time technical writer, I decided to stop wearing a watch so I could learn to trust myself and my internal guidance more directly. At first, I was rather fearful and uncertain about being late for or missing project meetings without my watch to tell me what time it was. Many times, what goes on in the first ten minutes of a meeting is the most important, and it was difficult enough to get three or four programmers to meet at the same time without me missing out on it!

So with a deep breath, I had decided that simply holding the intention would be sufficient and my inner self would nudge me at exactly the right moment. In the beginning I had a few bouts of sudden panic, thinking I'd worked right through a software demonstration or some other meeting. But sure enough, I wasn't really late even ONCE. For instance, in the middle of writing a chapter, I would suddenly get the urge to get up and KNOW it was time for the meeting, or I'd be on my way to the drink machine and run into the person I was scheduled to meet. Once, when I actually worked THROUGH the time a meeting had been scheduled, the meeting itself had been canceled at the last minute!

At first it took a little getting used to trust myself in this way, trusting that it really could be this easy and wasn't something to worry about. In this case, as I let go of effort and struggle and the belief that I had to "be on guard" by checking my watch all the time, I gradually got used to letting my inner self take care of the reminders.

In my example, the fear that came up was that I'd be late or forget an appointment and negatively impact my productivity or writing career. Somehow these stakes, although they seemed serious enough to me at the time, can seem much LESS serious than the risk of losing a love or of not being able to pay your bills. The important thing to remember here, though, is that there is fundamentally no difference in these situations: each drama is about releasing our fears, turning our focus on what we WANT, and trusting our creative spontaneous Selves to get us there in the easiest way possible.

In many cases, our inner guidance has access to details about the current circumstances that we weren't even consciously aware of and guides us accordingly; it's a sort of cosmic efficiency. For instance, when I had "missed" the meeting that was canceled, the inner self just let me keep working on my writing, without interrupting me to gather my materials and travel to the meeting room in the other part of the building. My intention had been to go to the meeting, but my inner guidance knew it wasn't necessary.

Of course when it comes to trusting our inner selves and releasing our fears, our intuition helps us accomplish this only when we are ready or "strong enough," although that will mean different things to different people. Although the methods that our inner guidance uses may be a little "unfamiliar" to our habitual patterns of control and effort and predictability, we learn that we CAN trust our impulses.

45

Can Asking Include Pain?

(by Susan James)

You've heard it said "ask and it is given." What we need to understand is that we are not asking with our words, but the asking is with our vibration.

The "asking" is about that "desire" that burns within us. That desire that burns within us is asking.

SO—even in our pain, EVEN in our belief that we're not getting what we want, or might not EVER get what we want, our "desire" or our "asking" is STILL within it.

So—EVEN in the most negative contrasting experiences, there is STRONG ASKING as PART of that vibration. If the asking could be pure and not couched in the belief that it will not happen, the answer would come to you right then. There's something about turning the negative declaration into a verbal asking that softens the resistance in our moment.

This is a little clarity, because we confuse exactly what "asking" is. We do not "ask with our words." We are always asking with our vibration. (Feeling behind the words) But when we ask with our words, it lowers the resistance, which causes the asking that we are doing to match our vibration and with our desire to now be satisfied.

In that moment that you turn your declarative statement into a positive asking, your vibration will shift.

Two Primary methods of shifting energy:

A)   Turning the declarative (negative) statement into requests or asking.

B)   Writing out your intentions in an affirmative manner.[7]

---

[7] *Source: Abraham-Hicks Publications. Web-site: http://www.abraham-hicks.com, J&E Hicks, San Antonio, TX*

46

Burger King & Manifesting

(by Susan James)

This is how easy and good it is supposed to be.

1. *You drive up to the speaker box at Burger King.*

2. *You tell the speaker box what your desire is.*

3. *You think about your Whopper and heading home and yummy stuff.*

4. *As you are heading to the pickup window, you think of something else.*

5. *You pass the window, and the Whopper is tossed in your car, and it's even better than you thought, and they made a mistake and gave you two instead of one!*

It is that easy. Have it your way!

47

One Foot In and One Foot Out—What Will You Miss?

(by Susan James)

There is some "stuff" that you want: Love, Money, Love, Peace, Joy, Love, Prosperity, Health and Love.

Do you have one foot in and one foot out?

> *I choose…But will it come?*
> *I choose…But how will it come?*
> *I choose…But I want it to come this way!*
>
> *I choose…But I have to wait for this step first.*
> *I choose…BUT, BUT, BUT, BUT, BUT.*

All that you choose is made of "love stuff," but you may not be ready to hear that yet. You want your stuff!

Here is the good news in the new energy; you do not have to wait. We are embarking upon wonderful new energy that makes waiting, as you know it, nonexistent.

Everywhere you look, you are being told "verbalize and visualize." Here is a fact: we have help all around us in the forms of what we humans call Guides, Angels, God, nonphysical, "all that is…" But they are astral. They know what we want and need Spiritually because that is what they are. But for the human physical stuff, we need to tell them exactly what we need and desire. The way we tell them is in the form of the end result, and we then do not suggest how we want it done, other than in "the best possible way" and with "ease," etc.

So what is the end result? You think of exactly what you are desiring and think of yourself as already having it. You do not pray for peace; you are thankful that you have it. You do not pray for dollars, you are thankful that they are here, and how you feel knowing that.

Your choice is: you can have one foot in the "work/action" mode and the other in the "verbalize/visionary" mode—and your manifestations will be slower in coming.

A key ingredient in the "new energy" is "vocal." You have to say it Out Loud. Just thinking the thoughts is not enough anymore.

You verbalize by saying "this is so great, this thing that is mine, and this is how much I enjoy it in my life" etc.

Now Do It!

48

And Something Else

(by Susan James)

Lets assume you have stuff in your life that you do not want. You have made a conscious decision to take control of the design of your life by using the tools of "creating on purpose."

You need to get this into your brain and your heart NOW. If you talk and vent about the stuff you do not like in your life, you will only bring more stuff into your life that you do not like.

It is the Law of Attraction. It works when you are venting about what you do not want, and it works when you are expressing what you do choose for your life.

The whole point is YOU are choosing in each moment. YOU YOU YOU. What are you choosing?

Have an Incredible Weekend! **AND CHOOSE FOR YOURSELF!**

Love Susan

49

Turning Things around

(by Susan James)

1. Find the positive aspects of this situation.

2. Tell the Universe that I AM releasing it to them.

3. Ask for help.

4. *The Top three the most important!*

5 Envision a situation where everyone is Happy and everything turns out all right.

6. My gift from this is...

7. Everything does workout just fine if I remember to ask for it and allow it to come.

8. My job is to set my tone.

9. Expect the best from others, be O.K. because you only have a limited vision.

Love Susan

50

Loving Allowance

(by Susan James)

This is the Law of Allowance: loving who you are in every NOW.

1. *When resistance or lack appears, no matter how small, become very quiet and love "it"; "love" the resistance, love the negative feeling/thought, and "allow" it to be there.*

2. *You love this negative moment, because it gives you a "reminder" to go inward. Be thankful for this reminder, for inward is where the transformation is.*

3. *Each negative feeling is there to tell you to go inward, and for this reminder be thankful.*

4. *Inward is where the transformation is, your "allowing" of it all. For this reason, bless the negative feeling in that moment for reminding you to go inward.*

5. *So be in loving allowance of all facets of you, even the resistance, the negative moments, and in doing so you have CHANGED IT ALL!*

This exercise will change and transform you by loving the negative immediately.

Love Susan

Schools of Thought

(by Susan James)

There are various schools of thoughts/views on how to best handle those moments of angst, depression, anger and/or anxiety.

They usually fall within these categories—and I use "usually" loosely.

1. *I feel this way, and I will move through it, just feeling this way, until it is gone.*

2. *I feel this way, and I will move through it, and while I am moving through it I will tell others how I am feeling so maybe they can help, but I'm going to spew, regardless.*

3. *I feel this way. How can I move through this now? What takes me out?*

4. *I feel this way; it is temporary, but as of this moment I intend otherwise.*

Where various individuals fall within this, this is a tell-tale sign of their place in their own evolvement. We all have hit the various stages, even me, at one time or another. But you get to choose how long you stay there and how quickly you get to the stream of abundance, joy, bliss, etc.

I write this essay, however, strictly from the level of "energy." Energy and how and where you move it, and to whom.

When you are experiencing those "low energy" vibrations, you have the choice to keep it to yourself or send that same "low energy" to others, which is what happens when you spew it.

Now there are many folks who have ingrained within themselves the higher frequencies. They have done the pivot dance, they have made themselves firm in their own tone, and most likely your spewing will not affect them, or if they feel that they are vulnerable, they know not to read or listen to your stuff.

However, there are many new folks among our ranks who know nothing of manipulating anyone else's energy, much less their own, and anyone offering "lower energy" needs to be aware of the sensitivity of others. These others absorb the lower energy fields that began with the spewing of others, and then they pass it on, and yada, yada, just like tossing a pebble across a pond. It causes a ripple effect within the lives of others, as well as the Universe at large.

In other words, now that we know what we know, if we are going to "infect" others, which energy are we going to infect them with? We ALL get to choose.

We are—no, that is incorrect—WE HAVE been given tremendous tools in this "new energy." This is where our attention is best placed if we want to create our dreams, our heaven on Earth. On top of that, as we learn and know these things, we then have the responsibility to know how to best use energy, whether we are coming from a low dense place or a high vibration place.

In the upcoming essays of "Manifesting 101 & Beyond" we will be getting more and more into the new energy, and what it means for your life. All of us—YOU and Me—are in for such a glorious time, and the ride, at least for me, has not been too shabby to this point.

Always, My Heart Is Yours,
Susan

52

It Just Doesn't Make Sense

(by Kristen Fox)

I've tried to understand conscious creation from a rational angle. Yeah, I know, but I had to try, or at least it seems that way. But you know, some things just don't make sense. Like a friend who lost three pairs of sunglasses over the year, only to have them all reappear in one day: two in her purse and one on the front seat of her car. Or my other friend who manifested two very specific, and exactly the same, kitchen utensils where they weren't before. And the can opener that disappeared from a drawer in my kitchen, only to reappear there a few minutes later. Why did the sunglasses all come back THEN? Why TWO kitchen utensils? Why did the can opener disappear as I was about to open a can of tuna for lunch, and then come back five minutes later?

See, the trouble with creations like this, now that we're really paying attention to them, is that they "make no sense." I have spent lots of time trying to make up REASONS for these things. Maybe I did something in the meantime, while I was looking for the can opener, that was somehow important. Or maybe I just got to experience the flexibility of reality and the can opener was just the object I happened to be focusing on in the moment. But then, what's the symbolic significance of a can opener? Maybe my first friend had really been wanting to wear a pair of sunglasses. Maybe my second friend wanted to be able to cook in tandem with her significant other.

But as many reasons as I come up with, I've got even more questions which lead me to believe that this conscious creation stuff is NOT a system at all, or at least not one born of predictability.

That seems obvious when I see it in writing, but when implementing the ideas in physical reality, my old training steps back and says, "You want me to WHAT?" and "What just happened here?"

I do think that many of the questions we have about conscious creation make us look closer and closer at ourselves, at who we are, what we choose to think and focus on, what we are doing, and why we are here? And even if the physical events don't make sense to us, our experience of the events themselves are usually exactly right-on, according to our desires and growth. But now, back to physical reality.

Most of us grow up learning that physical reality is supposed to make sense. But "making sense" really means that it is understandable to our senses, which conscious creation mostly DOESN'T—not according to our USUAL interpretations of sense data, in any case. Many of us grew up in the era of scientific advancement and try, albeit unconsciously, to understand conscious creation through that belief system.

Reasons

A few years ago, I consciously and deliberately set about creating a new car for myself. It was an entire month before the insurance check came through for my previous car that was "totaled" in a collision. Why a month? I can say that during that time I really DID figure out what I wanted in a new car and decided I wouldn't settle for anything else, and that I ended up creating exactly the car I chose. I can say that I "learned" a lot during that month about what it felt like to drive a rental, what "owning" a car meant to me, etc. If I spent even more time thinking about it, I could come up with even more rational reasons—rationalizations—of why my new car creation happened the way it did. After a while, however, I discovered that the more reasons I wanted to find, the more I would create.

However, if I look behind the reasons and to the pattern of my thoughts that were CREATING the reasons, I'd understand a lot more about myself. The fact that I felt REALLY uncomfortable with NO REASONS was a big clue. My inner self was telling me that I would have my new car—no problem—and sometimes I even believed it! <grin> In the meantime, I fussed about this, complained about paperwork, refocused my thoughts on what I wanted, and then did it all again. Most of the time I was anxious, or at least dissatisfied with my current state of car-lessness, even though my daily patterns went on pretty much as usual.

And, even more frustrating to my habitual approach, there was ABSOLUTELY NOTHING I could do to hurry the process of getting my insurance payment; it was entirely out of my hands. I tuned in and asked myself what to do and heard, "Nothing.Go have fun." But did I? Of COURSE not! I worried, and thought about it, and rolled it around inside my head, and talked to friends. I even called the insurance company a few times, but was never able to get in touch with the right people and was only able to leave messages. It just made no sense.

Facing Up

Stepping back, I can see that trying to make sense out of creation is like trying to fit a square peg in a round hole, while repeating to yourself, "But it doesn't fit!" and then trying it again, with the same results, and then wondering why you're frustrated.

I finally admitted to myself that the old system of being able to explain things no longer works, and the more I tried to MAKE IT work, the more frustrated I became. But I'd relied on it for so long that when things didn't make sense, I felt like I'd been doing something WRONG. Things seem out of whack and out of control and THAT'S just GOT to stop! But it doesn't. I KNOW I'm "shifting" and I KNOW things are changing, but sometimes that just made me feel all the more clueless about what to do about any of it.

And, of course that's where trust comes in. I started out knowing the validity of the idea of having an inner self that knew a lot more of what was going on, but I never really relied on it before—at least not like I am now. The bigger the creation, the more outside your usual perimeter of experience your desired creation is, the more you must trust your inner self to guide you along, because—say it with me, "It just doesn't make sense."

You see, our old sense-based belief system cannot guide us as we once believed it did. I'm sure most of you are QUITE aware of that yourselves. Our expectations are now breaking free of the step-by-step progress that our egos had all planned out for us. We must turn to our inner selves to guide us.

Creating Outside the Lines

Conscious-creationally speaking, it's easy to trust and let go when we want to create, for instance, a nice pair of purple socks. We tune in, accept the socks into our reality, and then live our lives until they run into us, and then we say, "Oh, here they are!" and we smile and laugh.

What I see happening to many people I know right now is that they're all reaching for a lot more in their lives. Our hearts are just BURSTING to experience our deepest and highest desires. Reaching for these desires is a process by which we expand beyond our habitual belief system, and into trusting "the unseen" or inner self. As we move more into the realm of conscious creators, we begin to see situations not as problems or solutions, but simply as "situations." We don't have a problem and then solve it, we have one situation, and then next, linearly speaking, we create a new and different situation. We don't get stuck reacting to the initial situation that we didn't feel we enjoyed; we create from our heart centers.

And when we create from our heart centers instead of reacting to the events in physical reality, strange things start to happen. We break out of the linear step-by-step frame of mind and take great leaps that are simply not comprehensible through the rational mind alone. In striving to understand these leaps that seem to happen to us, we open up to the greater part of who we are—that magical part that's always been there for us, even when we weren't aware of it. As we become more aware and expanded, our goals, what we desire to create for ourselves in physical reality, also become more expanded. We grow into our dreams as much as they grow into us.

It still doesn't make sense, but eventually that stops bothering us as much, because we know that it's not sense and logic that defines our new framework of being, if anything really can, but JOY and MAGIC and SPONTANEITY. The more trust we experience, the more we can let go of the old now-dysfunctional rules we used to live by and the bigger life we can experience.

During this strange process of transformation, I have experienced many a doubt and fear, but that physically-focused part of me has discovered many things. First, it is not the ego that creates through effort, it is the total self that creates through allowing. I can describe it like this: I tune into my inner self and find myself really resonating with an idea or thought, and I find myself feeling really good and thinking, "That would be cool!" Then, I assume that's something my inner self is going to create for me to experience (just playing with the illusional "divisions of self" here) and will lead me there in the best way possible. There's no effort involved; joyous impulses and intuitions will be my guide.

But what if you choose the goal of, for example, manifesting a new car for yourself, and suddenly find yourself without any car at all and needing a bus pass? Is the creation not working? That's what the old belief system would say, but that belief system is only taking a small portion of factors into the equation. So when your current situation doesn't fit into the confines of how you're USED to seeing the world, no matter how much you think it over or worry about it, you must trust that the inner self knows what it's doing.

The Misrepresentation of the Rational Mind

One of the things that helped me to understand this better was the realization that I had been using the term "rational mind" without really knowing what I meant by it. The term "rational mind" is one many of us throw around quite often, but what IS the rational mind? How have we been habitually using an unconscious definition to frame our thinking? And who does the thinking? Do we "think" the way we THINK we think? So many questions from two such seemingly innocuous words.

First, what IS the rational mind? I believe (an interesting word to use here, too! <G>) that the rational mind is that "part" of us that is focused in physical reality. It is the part of our expanded consciousness that allows us to EXPERIENCE events in physical reality. The beliefs internalized by the rational mind are what enable the rational mind to focus on specific experiences. When we say we "believe" in something, we mean our physically focused selves have decided to experience this situation in physical reality. A belief is a specific focus.

Beliefs limit our experience,but a less judgmental look at that phrase might give us: "Beliefs FOCUS our experiences." When we are children, we accept the belief systems of our parents, until we begin expressing individuality which our parents' belief systems do not permit. Then, theoretically, we discard the beliefs that prevent us from experiencing our chosen situations and accept beliefs that DO allow us to experience our chosen situations, or desires.

Thus, the rational mind is a filtration system to focus our attention. When we want to experience a red light, we place a red filter in the stream of light, and perceive that red part of the light in physical reality. In this metaphor, we are the stream of light, our beliefs are the filters of our light, and our rational minds are what experience the red light through our emotions. If we can think of physical reality as resonating in a certain range of vibration, we can think of the rational mind the same way. A thousand things may be going on around us, but we see what we expect to see and are open to seeing, according to our belief systems.

The reason this whole topic came up was because I'd recently found myself in a discussion that argued "rational mind" versus "intuitive mind," which seemed completely circular, opposite, and pointless. Questions were asked such as, "But are we supposed to throw rational thinking out the window and just trust out intuition?"

It was a good question, but I knew there wasn't a simple "yes" or "no" answer there. Why do these questions always sound like it's the rational mind OR the intuitive, and why did we see these two as a duality? Something wasn't quite right. Then I started wondering about all of the things we unconsciously attribute to the rational mind but are—shocker—not really a function of the rational mind at all.

For instance, as I discussed earlier, when we say something "makes sense," what we are really saying is that we understand it in such a way that it fits into our current belief system. As we grow, and as our beliefs change, different things "make sense" to us at different times. Societally, however, many of us have adopted the rules of logic and scientific methodology as our belief systems, and yet as we experience more events that don't "make sense" in that system, we are forced to either deny our experiences to maintain the status quo or release a jealously-guarded belief that we have taken for granted, probably for our entire lives.

We have also been assuming that any thought or belief that "makes sense" to us is "a rational thought." What, then, is an irrational thought? A thought that has NOT been incorporated into your current belief system and experienced in physical reality. As a culture, however, we have applied interesting connotations to these words. "Rational" means workable, while "irrational" means non-workable, and we tend to believe that the line between these two has been chiseled into stone.

Let's try an example. I recognize a desire for a drink. In order to experience drinking, we unconsciously look to our current belief system to provide the answer of what action to take. Using a current mass belief system, we would then accept and follow the impulse to get up, go to the refrigerator, and pour ourselves a nice, cold glass of our favorite beverage, believing that this is the way to get a drink.

However, when we become aware of our current belief system as just beliefs and not the be-all-and-end-all of physical reality, we suddenly become open to other possibilities. What happens when we suddenly recognize a desire for a drink, but DON'T experience an impulse to go the refrigerator? What if we experience a desire to walk outside instead? The impulse to walk outside is NOT "rational" or "physically-verifiable in the moment," because it doesn't fit into the conscious set of beliefs under which we are operating. It is NOT logical, it hasn't already been proven that walking outside your home will get you a drink, you can't prove it from where you are, and yet there's the impulse. If we follow the impulse, we find that a friend is just arriving with a nicely chilled bottle of white wine. In following an impulse in physical reality, that is, acting in a rational or sense-oriented path, we discover that our "irrational" impulse was "accurate" after all, even if we couldn't see this and simply had to TRUST ourselves to follow the impulse.

What this example is showing is that we are expanding our ability to recognize impulses beyond those of the mass belief system. No physical evidence would support the idea that "going outside" would provide a drink, and yet it turned out to be accurate. This is the point where we can either decide to deny our experience or accept the new information into our belief system. Sometimes we hold conflicting beliefs for a long time, and unconsciously, before we resolve them. Every belief conflict we experience is an opportunity for growth beyond our current understanding.

And why isn't it rational mind versus intuitive mind? Because the intuitive mind doesn't just focus on what's going on INSIDE. The intuitive mind or inner guidance takes the information your rational mind gathers from physical reality AS WELL AS information that is not physically evidenced in the present, and then blends them together in order to form an answer or impulse which is more complete and in harmony with ALL relevant information.

Thinking

Now, to the idea of "thinking" itself. When we say we "think," we are actually saying that we "believe" something. "Logical thinking" generally means that the thought that answers the original question-thought can be followed in a linear, step-by-step and "physical" manner. We usually use the phrase "rational thinking," referring to a thought which falls into the currently accepted belief system.

But as I mentioned before, I don't think we "think" in the way we think we think. We've trained ourselves to consider thinking under the same blanket as logic and rationality. But "thinking" isn't something that our physical focus, our rational mind, actually DOES! Thoughts exist independently of the rational mind. We attract thoughts into our experience by our desire for them—magnetism. For instance, I have a question and the answer comes, either through my own experience of the answer-thought, or perhaps some-one else tells me the answer-thought. Every thought we "think" is really an inspiration from our creative selves, filtering through our belief system. Sometimes we can even watch ourselves go through a process of filtering out the desired solution by only choosing the thoughts that WOULD be logically and physically-provable—which may present the illusion of "thinking" that we are used to perceiving. We call this "thinking" instead of "allowing" or "trust-ing" the answer to come, but there is essentially no difference.

Trusting ourselves is just another way of saying that even though my experi-ence or information from my inner self doesn't fit into the current belief sys-tem, I will not deny the validity of it; instead, I will discover what area of my current belief system is wishing to change to allow this information to exist consciously for my rational focus.

The key thing to remember here is that all of this "new age" stuff isn't really "new." We are ALREADY following our impulses. The difference is that now we are allowing ourselves to follow impulses outside what would be considered "rational." I have been in a lot of situations that have required me to open to new information because my old understandings held no answers for me but fear and denial. Most of our struggle is in the adjustment of releasing old, well-worn beliefs for new beliefs that aren't as well accepted or understood by oth-ers around us. You see, intuition is a one-person job. No one else can tell you or show you or explain to you what your intuition is saying.

This is why the best "new age" information tells each person to live in joy and conscious intention, and be an example, helping each person find their OWN inner voice and expressing it. That's the only way it can really be done. Once again, when we inevitably compare this way of being with our old belief sys-tem, we find that no effective comparison can really be made. Sense informa-tion versus the combination of sense and "non-sense" information.

So...

> Just because it makes no sense doesn't mean it doesn't work.
> Just because you can't explain it doesn't mean it's not real.

Just because you ARE "making sense" doesn't mean you're NOT following an impulse.

and

Just because I believe this article is true doesn't mean it's not just a bunch of good "reasons" I created in order to make it easier for me to trust my intuition!<grin>

End

53

Introduction to the Beyond Phase

(by Susan James)

In Manifesting 101 & Beyond we still discuss the Laws of Manifesting. However, it is the "Beyond" part that this next series will focus on more purely.

It is the "beyond" part that we will push the envelope on our selves and our current belief—or lack of it. We will see how we feel about "unlimited thinking" and "outrageous thinking," and determine if we are willing to test ourselves here, to bring about the changes desired in our lives—on all levels.

These words have lost their luster and meaning for many: "Love, Light, Trust," but we find in the New Energy there is a new level of definition, of Vibration, that we must become familiar with to further evolve in humanness, as well as in our Spiritual selves.

Just what is this new energy? To touch briefly, it is about "directing energy" with our thoughts. It is about leading our lives from our nonphysical (Spiritual) side, and knowing the difference. It is to know so "purely" the communication that we receive from Spirit—and to trust it.

Are you yet at the point where you can "let go" of all that is "logical" and let Spirit guide you?

So I ask you, are you ready for the purity of information available to you? Are you ready to trust it? Are you ready to "think" like a Spirit?

> *Does this mean you have to become a monk? NO.*
> *Does this mean you have to mediate and say OM? NO.*
> *But what does it mean? You'll have to stay tuned to find out.*

54

Must We Meditate to Hear Our Higher Selves/Spirit?

(by Susan James)

Spirit speaks to us when our "self" is occupied. By being occupied, this does not mean running around frantic in our day, trying to get our stuff done. You will not hear anything.

Your "self" can be moved out of the way for Spirit to speak with you simply by doing menial things, things that you enjoy, or tasks that are simple that you perform. For instance, you can hear your higher self while reading book, while gardening, while taking a walk.

Spirit does not limit its ways of speaking to us by setting prerequisites of our sitting in a lotus position, although many do enjoy mediation for different reasons, and not to negate that, as many prefer the quiet and solitude that this discipline brings.

My "first" real noticeable moment of "block of thought energy" came to me in the shower several years ago. It was clear and pure—of that there was NO question. Then the hunger for more began.

The point being that many folks assume that they will not be able to have a close connection to the All That Is/God/Higher Self unless they can sit still for a period of time and block out the world. Nothing is further from the truth.

The other important part of this equation is that we MUST ASK.

Our God/Higher Self wants to communicate with us and help to guide us, but we MUST TELL "them/it" that we desire this communication. Then it is done. Spirit then sends inspiration. Are you "open" enough to hear, and then if you hear, will you LISTEN?

55

What Happens to Your "Thought" When You Are Done with It?

(by Susan James)

> *You have a thought...I am losing weight.*
> *You have another thought...I'll never lose weight.*
> *You have a thought...I have gobs of money.*
> *You have another thought...But I don't have enough to buy this thing.*

This is what happens per the above:

1. *You have negated your potential creation. (This one by now should be obvious to you)*

2. *All of your thoughts are "things." When you think/say, I'll never lose weight—that thought goes out into the Universe. It then is picked up by other people who also believe that they will never lose weight. So you have helped the folks with "weight issues" stay where they are. They, by their own use of the "Law of Attraction," have attracted your energy as it relates to their weight loss issues. So what you think is what you get, and what you think, other folks get as well. That is how powerful thought is!*

3. *On the "positive end," anyone "out there" thinking "Money comes to me easily"—if YOU are also thinking "money comes to me easily," you then attract someone else's thought to match your own—and the power is multiplied.*

Summary: This is how you change YOUR world, and this is also how YOU change THE world! With your vibration, with your frequency, i.e., with your thoughts!

56

The Wisdom Loft

(by Susan James)

Question:	*What is the worst thing you can do to attract to you want you desire to manifest?*
Answer:	*Worry*
Question:	*I have something in my life that I do not want.*
Answer:	*Discontinue sending energy towards it.*
Question:	*Is there a secret to communicating with my higher self?*
Answer:	*Yes, the secret is to ASK for this communication. Just ASK!*

57

Needles or Noodles

(by Susan James)

You are a needle. The Universe is trying to move its power through the eye of your needle.

As you allow more of this power to flow through you, all things, which you consider to be good, flow to you.

As you allow more power, more power is available to you. Why would you "want" this? It is why you came: to remember WHO YOU ARE!

Is the eye of your needle open?
Is it opening more and more?
Or are you pushing a wet noodle with no power at all at your back?

58

Reminder: The Dudd!_The "Do/Un-Do Dance"

(by Susan James)

> *I want, BUT I can't have.*
> *I choose, BUT It will never happen*
> *I am rich, BUT I am Poor.*
> *I am thin, BUT I am not.*

Also called "The BUT Dance." Whatever you call it, it equals "zero" movement towards your desire. It negates your original intention. YOU ARE STUCK!

FIX IT, FIX IT, FIX IT!

59

The "How to" of Getting What You Want Is Changing!

(by Susan James)

It used to be that we could do this "surrender" and "letting go" thing to God, and things would just seem to workout.

Of course, for a person to get to that point in that relationship with "himself" is quite wonderful.

But that is the "old energy" way.

The Planet and the Universe are changing. It has been changing, and this is what the "New Energy" is about.

The New Energy is about a "handshake with Spirit/God/Universe."

In the "old energy," we could program our "thought" patterns alone, and things could change.

In the New Energy, the "verbalization" is paramount. It is the verbalization that is the handshake. We tell Spirit what we require, and then we just let it go. We don't ask, we don't plead, we don't ask if it's ok; we tell Spirit what we need and require. We tell Spirit the end result of what we require; we do not tell Spirit how to bring it to us.

What is the main difference here, in this principle between the old and new energy?

The main difference is that we are to see our Spiritual help on the other side. (Angels, Guides, God) as our best friends. A friend, that just because you asked, you know they will deliver, and you don't have to call to make sure, you don't have to follow up, you just know you have placed it in trusting hands, and simply because you asked it is yours.

Your best friend "here," (in the physical) cannot read your mind, so you have to tell them what you need. It is the same now in the new energy. You have to verbalize.

This is the "Co-Creation." This is a "new" gift.

But YOU must ask out loud. Spirit needs to hear the verbalization, and it needs to come back into your ears verbally. That is the completeness of the handshake.

I have a small example here, and then a much larger example later in this issue.

At one time I had a payment that was due, and I had no idea where the funds were going to come from. This was when I began learning and integrating the "old vs. new" energy thing. I decided in that moment to test this out.

So I said, "Ok, Universe, I need this amount of money, by this date, but I prefer to have it by "this" date! Now I am testing this with you. I want to know that this works. So SHOW me!" And then I forgot about it—on purpose. I did not affirm it further.

The funds arrived EARLY! I just smiled and I said,"Okay, I can do this. I understand." Now I use it for any and all situations, circumstances and events.

Regarding the money issues. Spirit is astral. Money is not astral. It means only energy to Spirit. That is why you have to be specific. Tell them how much you need and require. Then let it go. It shows up. But you must verbalize and talk to Spirit and recognize the place of Spirit in your life.

It is further written somewhere that the Angels went to God and said,"God, we have nothing to do. Humanity will not talk to us and tell us what they need. We cannot intervene without invitation. So they go on in distress, when if they would just ask us out loud, they would have bounty in their lives."

So do the handshake; test it, it works.

Susan

60

The $3,000 Story

(by B. W.)

I had been practicing envisioning and affirmations for quite some time, but I had never really let go. Not really. I always held on a little "just in case." NOT ANYMORE…

On a Monday, I knew that I needed another $3,000 for Friday's payroll. I had been really closing up my energy, thus not allowing money to flow freely the past week or two. But NOW I REALLY NEEDED MONEY. I had just billed out $19,000, but knew that this would not get to the customers and back to me in time for payroll on Friday. The previous Friday, I had also billed out to one customer who was to pay on receipt. I thought this customer would pay within a couple of days, but on Monday when I called her office said that she had left on Saturday for California.

I began to panic. I called a friend of mine, and together we voiced what I wanted—OUT LOUD. We told my Angels/Guides/God exactly what and when. We said "I want $3,000 by Thursday at the latest. Then I said "OK, guys—I now give you the whole thing. I am done! It is yours, now you get this job done."

I got busy with other things that made me happy. I remained in my happy places until I was standing at the kitchen sink and I recognized my "old" thought pattern. You know the one that says, "Well, I could transfer money from savings or ask my father," and then a voice shot out of me so clear and so loud—"NO! NOT THIS TIME! I AM GOING TO GET THIS DONE MY WAY!" I have given it away to my Angels/Guides/God and they will figure it out! I have to stay focused on remaining happy.

So that is what I did. Wednesday came, and I had received about $1,200.00. I began to see that I can let them do their work. Thursday came, and I received another $5,300.00. OK, now this was fun! I had received a total of about $6,500.00 in all by Thursday, not to mention that Friday I received even more—and more…

Now you remember that customer who went to California? She was one of the customers who sent me a check. I have no explanation as to how it happened, for if I mailed her a statement on Friday late afternoon and she left town on Saturday morning and then mailed me a check (in the exact amount, which she could have not known unless she had the statement) to me on Monday from California (that's what the postmark said) and I received it on Thursday. She usually sends me payments within a couple of days, but this was truly amazing to me. There was no one at her house while she was away, so this is a miracle indeed…

So how do I believe? I JUST DO. There have been way too many things that have happened in my life that I have no explanation for in my physical existence.

I fell into the arms of my Angels/Guides/God. I remember this every time I think, *Now how am I going to do this or that*, my faith is very strong INDEED, and I am always looking forward to more miracles in my life!

In the end, the biggest lesson I learned is that when I intend and affirm for something OUT LOUD, and then I let it go—I step out of my Angels/Guides/God's way—they always do perfect work!

61

Have You Found Your Magic Wand?

(by Susan James)

At the end of this long corridor sits a chair—quite an exquisite chair. You were told that your magic wand is sitting in that chair. The magic wand was the key to all of your dreams coming true.
So quite naturally, this is something that you want: a magic wand!

However, you start down this corridor, and there are people along the hall-way—some that you know, some that you don't know. They are trying to keep you from your destination.

But you have been given a vision or a nudge or a simple understanding that if you could just get to that chair and that magic wand, then you could create your paradise, your utopia.

So you stop and you start, as friends and neighbors and acquaintances seem to act as though they do not want you to reach your destination.

They ask you where you are going. You tell them "To retrieve my magic wand." They tell you "It's fools gold! There is no magic wand. Stay here with us!"

You stop and you start time and again, but you have moved forward each time.

Finally, finally you reach the steps to your exquisite chair. You climb the steps. You face the chair—and the wand is not an actual wand.

It is your "Self worth." Your God/Self. With this, you are handed your utopia to create.

Susan

62

Abundance, But How?

(by Susan James)

We all want it. Some of us chase it until we understand that we don't have to chase it, and it just comes. But HOW?

That can get a little tricky if you're not willing to change a little—and for some, a lot.

How hard is the change? It, of course, depends on you.

The equation in most of the inspired literature that has been around for a long time, as well as the most recently inspired publications, have this simple equation for abundance.

Self worth+Peace=Abundance.

There are basically two ways to have abundance/prosperity in your life.

One: You can chase it…(I did that one already.)

Two: Or you can attract it to you. (I'm doing this one now.)

I won't write here about chasing it; that one 'hurt' too much. Too many oak trees that I had to knock into for that one.

So the bottom line key here is self worth. If you don't teach yourself that it's okay for you to take care of your own heart "first," then abundance has a problem finding its way to you. You are closed off from it.

The Universe works in an ebb and flow fashion, the give and take. If you are one who gives, and gives and gives, and gives—thinking you are doing a "good" thing—but you have trouble "giving" to yourself, you are slowing down, and in some cases shutting off the flow.

You also must be willing to receive, to keep your heart open to others giving to you. To being able to say "thank you" for this, instead of "No, you keep that."

Or a famous way of blocking the flow is that you "do and do and do" for everyone else "first," and if there is any time, money, or love left over, then maybe you will get some. We all know that usually YOU don't get any.

Part of giving to yourself is letting others give to you. But not only letting them give to you, but actually "enjoying" that someone has given to you without your feeling "guilty" or feeling like you need to reciprocate in some fashion. By not enjoying the receiving, you mess up the flow of the good back to you. If you cannot accept "simple" gifts in joy, how do you think the Universe can find a way to bring you the big stuff?

Along my own path, I have always been generous, and I had always worked on self worth, so I thought. But I got hung up in the "receiving" part, and did not know it. But the more I learned about abundance and the real flow of the Universe and gave my self permission to receive all good things—the joy always increased for my self, as well as the giver. When you have that, you have perfect flow. The better I got at that, the more the Universe poured its magic all over me. Then more joy came, and the giver received back in my acceptance and my self worth continued to grow, because I was giving my self permission to love my own heart. The circle for me just kept being completed instead of always just half finished, where the giver was not "given joy" in giving, because I was not in a good place to receive.

The circle is unbroken for me, and the Universe just keeps flowing good things.

Once you get really good at accepting from your "physical" friends and acquaintances, you then easily move that over to the "invisible spirit" of God/Universe and the Angels and Guides.

To think they want to give and give to all of us—all we have to do is accept it in joy, and more comes.

As I have said here many times, "We have been taught backwards, our way to joy and abundance." The road feels better once you understand and find the road.

I found it.

Open your heart to yourself, and just see what magic happens!

Love Susan

63

Take Money Away!

(by Susan James)

As we learn to use the energy of the Law of Attraction, sometimes the hardest thing to do is to measure where you are. The inspired literature says, "Look around you; that tells you how you are *vibrating*." In Universal terms, *vibrating* is your language to the Universe.

If you feel good, you are vibrating good things to the Universe and the Universe sends good things back to you. If you do not feel good, that's what can come back to you as well.

So lets use some examples: You want a new car. Are you trying to associate having a new car with the money it would take to purchase it: $30,000.00. Or are you trying to associate your self with simply having a new car?

Which feels better and more attainable to you? $30,000.00 or the new car?

You need to notice this, because it does make a difference. If you feel that attracting the money for the car is hard, then you shut off the flow. But if you can simply "think" about sitting in your new car, that is easier for you to "see" and feel, and your language to the Universe is in support of attracting your new car.

Lets assume you want a new career or livelihood or job. Are you seeing yourself in that new place, or are you trying to go for the money first? Which, then, will bring you the correct job? I have been really successful with this one myself, both off purpose and on purpose. More on that in another essay.

So many of our wants, needs, and desires can be more easily fulfilled if we take "money" out of the equation. If you think "I've got to have money to have this situation or thing," then you shut down millions of other ways that the Universe can bring it to you.

Keep your options open, and don't define your options; that is the job of the Universe.

Susan

64

Wake Up! Your Creating!

(by Kristen Fox)

What if I told you that everything you experience in physical reality is a reflection of who you are in each moment? That each experience, each person, each event, each object, is a projection of yours onto the screen of life, an expression designed to remind you of your incredible power as a Creator?

Let's say that each of us is a being of energy and that we each resonate or vibrate with our own unique signature vibration. These differences in vibration create our physical bodies differently, as well as our experiences and the thoughts that we entertain, and so you get what you vibrate! More simply, like attracts like, or, you get what you focus on. Not only are we an extension of our Whole Selves cleverly directing our focus onto the details of physical reality, but as we go about our lives, we are the ones who pick the perspectives and the probabilities that we live out by choosing what we focus on!

Now you might say that you could definitely see where SOME things reflect who you are, like that new car that you just bought, or that apple pie you just made, or the grinning child you just tickled, but certainly not EVERY-THING—especially those things in your life that you find at least somewhat disturbing. That's where the "becoming conscious" part fits in. If there's a part of your life that you are not happy with, that's probably a place where you have been creating haphazardly and are unaware that you're doing it. That is, you're sending out a certain vibration without your conscious knowing—like the background music piped in at your local grocery store, or the wallpaper in your kitchen, or the air that you breathe. These objects or experiences are all a part of your life, yet you may accept them as simply a part of the WAY LIFE IS, rather than a reflection of your personal symbology or vibration. One way to get a handle on this concept is to start looking at your life and the events you experience as you would interpret a nighttime dream. You'll never look at your shoes or your annoying coworker the same way again!

I remember the first time I became conscious of an assumption I'd made about "how life was." I was about 13 years old and had gone to a friend's house to stay the night. When they pulled out the extra bed and her mother made it for me, she put it together without a top sheet—just a bottom sheet, a blanket, and a pillow. I remember wondering if I should tell her that she forgot it, until I saw that my friend's bed was made the same way. This is a funny, but important, example. It wasn't until I met with this contrasting experience that I began to see the actual framework of beliefs (vibrations) in which I grew up. I was suddenly aware of the song being played in the background; I now saw the wallpaper, or at least peeked under the corner of it, as if for the first time. Talk about opening Pandora's box!

So how then was the fact that my bed at home was made with a top sheet a reflection of who I was or what I was vibrating? That's where our feelings about what we experience come into play. Contrasting experiences also allow us to see our own emotional reactions more clearly. Now what if I told you that "feeling bad" about something is not just a part of how life is, but a call to pay attention, because what you're choosing to focus on and experience in that moment is not aligned with who you really are? And what if I told you that "feeling good" is not just a part of how life is, but a call to pay attention, because what you're choosing IS aligned with who you are?

We feel good when our vibrations are aligned with what we're experiencing. But we feel BAD not just when our vibrations are NOT aligned with what we're experiencing, but when we alter our own vibration to match the discordant vibration of what we're experiencing. In essence, instead of being the director and setting our OWN tone to create in joy and alignment, we've become reactive to things and events we perceive OUT THERE. The ironic part is that we're the ones who created the experiences in the first place and just seem to have forgotten, and so we perpetuate the loop of projection and reaction until we decide to jump out of the cycle. At that point, we stop identifying ourselves with all the "stuff" out there and come back to our own centers, where it all starts.

The process of becoming aware of what we've been creating and then learning to consciously alter our own beliefs (vibrations) to create what we WANT can be one of the more challenging and psychological tasks of our time. Yet isn't that exactly what we came here to do in this time of awakening? We're given prophecies of doom, and dramatic situations to help shake us up and make us ask, "Isn't there something ELSE? Something BETTER? What are my other choices beyond FEAR?"

The more we let go of our habitual stance of focusing on fear as reality and instead look to love and joy and connectedness, the more we align with our own sense of personal integrity—the more we INTEGRATE and work WITH that divine aspect of each of us. Although our unconscious lives may have been created through a habitual focus in fear, our growing conscious awareness now knows it has the choice to choose love, where it once defaulted to fear. When we realize this, then we are truly free. Then that's how we vibrate, and how we create our new experiences in physical reality!

65

The Wisdom Loft

(by Susan James)

Question:	*How do I get what I want?*
Answer:	*Make a Decision, and do not waiver.*
Question:	*Is that "all," I have to do?*
Answer:	*One: State your intentions.*

(In present tense--"I have/I Am")

Two: Verbalize your intentions in the present tense.

Three: Take action when inspired. If you are "trusting and listening," you will be sent inspiration, ideas, synchronicity. Trust your intuition and discernment. This will move you in the direction of being in receipt of your goals/desires/intentions.

66

Mohammed Ali & My Boyfriends

(by Susan James)

Almost every day, I go for a 3-mile walk in the local park. I go to visit with the mallards and the baby ducks, and to keep my hips down. But I also use this time to move through stuff, or to ask for inspiration if I am in need of an idea or something.

Usually, one of my boyfriends shows up to share the walk with me. They range from bypass surgery to double-bypass surgery to triple-bypass surgery to my high school principal. My favorite park boyfriend is my high school principal, because he is more openly affectionate with me in public, and for some reason I really like that!<Grin>

I tell you this, to let you know, that I am much, MUCH younger than all of my boyfriends, but they bring a certain quality to my walks, in that they have seasoned stories to share. Charles has a walking stick and leans mostly on his car, and when he sees me coming, he stands in the middle of the road so there is no getting by this man!

Now notice that I am walking in the middle of the morning. That's when the "bypass boyfriends" can handle the heat better, but I have designed my life so I can just get up and go for a walk whenever it pleases me to do so. I have intended well.

Usually, as I enter the park I will say out loud, "OK, I intend to move through this issue and feel better by the end of the walk." 99% of the time, I am back to joy and balance when I do this, and I have peace over whatever the issue may have been.

One particular day, as I entered the park, my intention was this: "Bring me an idea for the next Manifesting 101, " and I began walking.

Within five minutes, my park boyfriend Joe Stone (great name, huh?) shows up. Now Joe is not one of the bypass boys; he simply has lived next to the park all of his life and has walked in the park for the past 20 years or so. He has taught me a lot about ducks and horses.

Anyway, we are saying our goodbyes in the parking lot, and he tells me a story about "Mohammed Ali," of how Ali was being interviewed about a Rolex Watch commercial he was doing (years ago), and how Ali was saying into the camera, "I love this new Rolex; in fact, I DESERVE 2 of them!"

Right then I knew. Who has done it better, this verbalizing stuff out loud, than "The Great One," or was it "I Am the Greatest"? And notice how he always used the word "I AM" as he made his statements about himself. That man was always "affirming" out loud. He was always intending good things for his life out loud. Even now, due to his advanced years and challenge, he is still affirming and very loving and very peaceful and very well taken care of.

He used his Intentions as his Magic Wand, and look at what he accomplished for himself, which then transferred over to his family and loved ones, and was quite an entertainment entity for many, not to mention the many jobs and careers that were made, due to his persona and product.

And just a reminder, I intended to have an idea for the next M101, and I not only got that, but I got more. Use your Wand! Your Intentions are Your Magic Wand!

Love Susan

67

It Just Falls at My Feet! (More On My Manifesting Story)

(by Susan James)

I had written "My Manifesting Story" a while back that went out to the newsletter subscribersand participants in one of my group focus intensives. This is an addendum to that story.

I sent out "Susan's Manifesting Story" on a Saturday evening, and then shut down the computer and went out. Sunday, I came in and turned on the computer and all kinds of good stuff was beginning to load in my E-mail.

I open a message from John. Excuse my expression but I am sitting there and I say out loud "Holy shit." John had received my manifesting story, and in return for something that I had helped him get clear on, he wanted to build me a professional web site—Free of charge NOW!

Now, for you who know more about Web-sites than I do, this may not be a big deal to you, but it is a HUGE big deal to me, and I won't bore you with the litany of reasons. But what I do hope that you see is this: having a really good web-site was one of my major "intentions."

Other than the deep gratitude spin I went into, there is a "Mechanics of Spirit" here. I had placed my intentions around having a web site, and that it would come to me in "ease & effortlessness." I attached no money issue to it at all. If I had attached money to it, then I would have shut off many other possible avenues of delivery of this Manifestation. I simply placed my intentions around it, with no expectations or requirements of how it would come—other than with ease and effortlessness.

I am amazed every day! I amaze myself every day, how this "stuff" all works, once you figure it out! Your Intentions and your Decisions are your magic wand!

Oh, and by the way, if you are saying, "OK, great Susan, for you, but..."

Please remember, I have had my days of *FEAR*. Where fear grabbed my heart and fear grabbed my stomach, and fear grabbed my mind. It does not happen anymore! I have done the "work," I have dropped my own "B.S." And how? By intending it to be so! I knew life was easier, and I knew that Magic and joy and happiness abound. I knew that all of my optimism and enthusiasm was not going to be enough to get me there. It had to be something else. That something else is learning about the Laws of Attraction and living them. Learning about the Law of Allowing and living it! Some of you are getting it; I know because you tell me. Some of you want to get it; I know because you tell me. Some of you already have gotten it and live it, and I know because you tell me! Just keep on, plant your feet and let no one steal YOU from YOU!

Susan

68

The Wisdom Loft

(by Susan James)

Question: *Does the "how to" really matter?*
Answer: *No*

Question: *How come the "how to" does not matter?*
Answer: *In order to accomplish something, you only must be "willing" to do whatever it takes to accomplish it. You must be "willing" to do whatever it takes. (And what you will find, is that it does not take nearly as much "action," as you may have thought, to bring you your desire or goal) BUT, you Must be "willing to do whatever it takes" to achieve this goal.*

Comment: *It is simply within the energy of the "willingness" that puts the Law of Attraction to work for you. The method, the "how to," is not important.[8]*

---

[8] *Source: "The Ultimate Secret to Getting Absolutely Everything You Want" by Mike Hernacki, Berkley Publishing, 1988. (Special Thank you to Lee Magnum for recommending this book to me almost a year ago!)*

69

The Mechanics of Spirit—Part One

(by Susan James)

Within the New Energy, there is a "Mechanics of Spirit." You have heard some of this before; in fact, this mechanics of spirit has been around over 2000 years, really much longer than that.

The DIFFERENCE NOW, in the New Energy, is that we are being "given" the knowledge—the "how to's" to USE this energy. We knew that it existed before, but we were not given the real spiritual logic to apply this knowledge. There is a difference between "human logic" and "spiritual logic." We were limited to our "human logic" application of the "mechanics of spirit," but no more.

It is similar to the "Aladdin's Lamp" story. The Lamp is there for us to use and to wish upon, but now we are being given the instructions of how to rub the lamp. But *OUR PART* is that we have to rub the lamp. Not only rub the lamp, but have full trusting that rubbing the lamp will bring us our over-all intentions. It is a tool. It is a gift. It is a spiritual gift that we are being given in the new energy.

So lets get to it:

1. *ASK & RECEIVE. (It's that simple)*

2. *Let's now break down the mechanics of Asking. This is the main mechanic of spirit—ASKING—and as you fine tune this, all that you consider to be good shows up.*

   a. *What is asking, and what is "asking aright?"*

b. *When you "ask aright," you ask with an Energy/Vibration that is so PURE that the LAW of Attraction has to MATCH it! It is Law.*

c. *How do you ask with pureness?*

d. *You break the asking down (the mechanics of spirit)*

Next is a conversation between the Universe and the ASKER for you to "see" better the "Mechanics of Asking."

Susan: *I want a red car.*
Universe: *Yes, you do.*

Session Over, you got what you wanted. (Susan got what she wanted, she "wanted" a red car, and the Universe said, "Yes, you are 'wanting' a red car." We are done here, are you happy?)

Susan: *No, I am not happy here...*
Universe: *Then clarify your question, we will help you.*

Susan: *I choose and intend a red car.*
Universe: *OK, here is one. A picture in a magazine.*

Session over you got what you were choosing. (Susan chose a red car, and the red car appeared in a magazine. Universe did its part.)

Susan: *I am still not happy here.*
Universe: *Clarify your question*

Susan: *I choose to have a red car, and I picture it in my driveway.*
Universe: *Okay, it is done. (Susan's Uncle George drives up in her driveway with a red car. It is his red car. Universe has again answered.)*

Susan: *This is not what I want!*
Universe: *Clarify your question*

Susan: *I choose to be the owner of my red car, under the best possible conditions. I own the pink slip, I keep the key to my red car in my pocket. I spill coffee all over my own new red car. I travel safely and have fun in my new red car. I am the proud owner of my brand new red car.*

Universe: *Here, then, is your red car that belongs to you, that you have the paperwork on, that you drive and spill coffee in, that you* *have the key in your pocket, because you are the proud owner of your new red car.*

SUMMARY: The Universe hears our vibration and MATCHES IT. If we are not specific and focused, then we get vague answers back, or interpret as unanswered requests. We have the power, we simply must fine tune and understand the mechanics of asking.

When our *ASKING IS PURE*, the *UNIVERSE MUST DELIVER., IT IS LAW.* When you break down your asking, intent and desire, you also increase the emotion. i.e., vibration around the asking. It is the *VIBRATION* that the Universe hears as language.

So go back and look at how you have been stating your intents and desires. If they are mousy, you get mousy results. The Universe Matches you according to your *ASKING*. It is Law. Make your *ASKING—PURE!*

70

The Mechanics of Spirit: Part Two—The Handshake

(by Susan James)

I can write about this, because I have and continue to experience it on a new level. Part of the New Energy and the Mechanics of Spirit is the actual "co-creation" with Spirit. It is "the handshake." It is the "rubbing of the lamp."

Many of us on the spiritual path have heard of Angels, Guides, God/Universe, All That Is. Then there are the folks who lean towards less "spiritual" terminology and more towards Universal Mind/Consciousness.

It does not matter what "name" you attach, or which perspective you tend to operate from. There is a "mechanics" involved in all of it. There are "tools & gifts" in all of it.

I most recently had been "using" as my tool "Guides." To use "Guides," as discussed in the "Kryon Papers" by Lee Carroll[9], helped me to expand my "understanding." I "need" to do this for myself, in the event that I hold any limiting thoughts about Angels. Using "guides," I have no current belief around, so I can make it up as I go along, and prove in evidence to myself new revelations.

This handshake—with Spirit, is with my guides. I have been able to turn over the trust that I had in "physical" human beings, whom I may trust with my life, to also now trust my guides with the same certainty.

---

[9] *Kryon materials by Lee Carol, can be found at this Web-site: http://www.kyron.com. The Kryon Writings, Inc., Del Mar, CA (Books 1–7)*

When you can bring yourself to that point, your world expands in many ways. You have a "nonphysical" counter part that "sees and knows" more than you do. They are here to "serve" us; they are here to do whatever makes us happy.

There is a joke that the Angels went to God and said that they were bored. Humanity would not ask them for anything. Man had all this stuff that the Angels could help with, but there is a rule in Heaven. Spirit cannot intervene unless it are asked. That statement is biblical. But there is a difference now from was first stated in the Bible. That is the Angels only job, to help "us."

We now are to "Tell"—yes, we TELL Spirit what we intend. We do not ask for "what is best," and "please get me out of this mess." We now tell the direction we would like to go to get us out of this mess. We do not tell Spirit how to do it. We simply state what we intend as an end result and let Spirit work out the ways and means and resources. We used to pray to God to help, and God would help, but it was more of a "one way" form of communication and not a partnership.

The fine line difference here now in the New Energy is that through our Intentions of what we would like the end result to be, we form a partnership with Spirit. Just like if you have a business partnership. You state your goal, and the two of you co-create the goal.

It is one of the New Energy Gifts. To use it, we must have "intent," and then we must believe that it "works." That our Guides/Spirit/Angels are our *best friends on the other side* and will do whatever they can to make us happy. That is their job!

Susan

Next Issue: "How to Begin This Spiritual Handshake"
Clue: YOU ASK!

71

The Wisdom Loft—So, What's the Difference?

(by Susan James)

Question: *What is the main difference between the partnership between Spirit now, and the other way of praying to God for our needs etc.?*

Answer: *Before, we "assumed" that we had no role in God's delivery of help or service. "It's in God's Hands" is the old way…*

The new way is that we can place the over-all end result intention in God's hands and let God/Universe/Spirit bring us our end result, without us limiting the Universe/God as to how the desired end result comes to us.

72

Your Absolute Power: The Handshake 'How-To'

(by Susan James)

We now in the new energy have a "fluid essence." We can use this "fluid essence" in manifesting our desires.

The innermost part of the atom contains an "invisible power/force." The name of this power/force:

Love

This invisible power of love actually defines the arc's orbits of the atoms, keeping them apart from each another, holding them at bay. Showing us that the "stuff" of which love is made is present at the "cellular level," the "atomic level," and also at the "astronomical level." Kryon refers to this love as having substance and being THICK. It is FLUID.

When you verbalize your intentions, that is when the FLUID FLOWS between that which is your essence as a piece of God and your essence as a human in lesson. "This is Critical!" (Direct quote from Kryon) "The verbalization of what you want and need must be out loud." No more as in the old energy you could think thoughts, and they might happen. NOW, for your absolute power you must verbalize as well. The "essence" of you NEEDS to hear the audible sound.

Let me tell you what I know from this in experience. I have been focusing on my "spiritual/consciousness aspects" of my growth. I have pages of affirmations and paragraphs that I read almost every day. I use them to move my energy, and since they are of a spiritual and unlimited nature as that, too, is my focus; I have no real preconceived ideas of any of it or what may or may not be next for me.

The next for me, and the more, and the next—just keeps coming. It is too incredible to spend time on here. But my point is that I taught myself a while back the importance of being audible in what I was stating as my intentions. They all have, and continue to, grow and flow towards me in leaps and bounds.

If you have a belief system that needs to be changed or expanded for you to move on, what better way than to tell the source of all belief systems that it is time to change, to move on, to move forward. You have this "liquid essence," what I like to call PURE LIQUID GOLD, just waiting for you to tell it what you "want" for your life. It is like the genie in Aladdin's Lamp.

This is the rubbing of Aladdin's Lamp; this is The Handshake with Spirit—the verbalization of your intent to your liquid essence that flows through you.

73

Intent Given for Your Higher Self

(by Susan James)

Over the past several essays, and for more to come, the topics have had a central theme of intent to bring your desires to you. An additional step, if you have not yet taken it, is to intend a full relationship with your higher self. Your higher self sees all, and from a different perspective than "you" do. Once you give intent for the marriage of your higher self and you, things take on a different perspective. You are guided differently, because you are guided from a higher place.

Part of this guidance is in the awareness of the synchronicity that is sent your way, to bring you more of your overall stated intentions for your life experience. Your higher self shows you the answers that you seek. It is the partnering with Spirit. Spirit wants to talk to you as a partner, but you must give intent. It will not happen without you verbalizing intent. Spirit cannot partner with you fully without invitation.

What better partner to have in your life or in your business than your higher self, who sees from above and can help you bring to you exactly what you state through your INTENT.

74

A Question of Rightness

(by Jeri Noble)

What if every choice you'd ever made turned out to be the most "right" of all possible choices? What if in the future, looking back on your life, you were able to see that no matter how badly it may have seemed you had chosen, in the long run you'd done exactly the right thing?

It can be difficult to accept our own rightness. It seems that there are so many possibilities, so many choices, that we sometimes just have to guess at the answer. But if we were to assume that there is something within us that does know the answers, always gets it right, wouldn't that improve our odds for success? Just from the viewpoint of increased self-confidence, there would be improvement.

The good news is that it isn't just increased self-confidence that makes the difference. In metaphysics, there is a principle which states that there is a Universal Mind, or Consciousness. This Universal Mind does have all the answers, and we're connected to it. In fact, we are an extension of it. When we allow ourselves to consciously connect with it, miracles happen. Life flows better, we have a far better idea of what we're doing, and there's a sense of Universal cooperation.

I'm not promoting any particular religion here, since most of them incorporate some variation on this theme. The science of metaphysics allows us to utilize this spiritual phenomenon and work with it. Interestingly, it doesn't seem to violate any other philosophical principles if we truly explore it. As a matter of fact, it seems to strengthen our personal belief systems, making them far more accessible.

Practice with this technique of accepting one's own rightness can lay a lot of old ghosts to rest. This is because the guilt and self-doubt which accompany any assumption that we've been wrong only inhibit our effectiveness. At the very least, we can believe that we're in the process of learning, not in the process of screwing up.

Within each of us is a core of rightness. We have the right to be here, to live our lives, and to accept that we are loved. We also have the right to our own choices. If we can live our lives from the belief that somehow we're doing it right, rightness happens. It's a metaphysical truism that what we hold in consciousness is what manifests for us in reality.

Go ahead. Be right.

Read more about Jeri on the Bio page!

75

The Sword in The Stone/Intent

(by Susan James)

Deepak Chopra[10] makes this statement: *"Intention is a force of nature, just like gravity."* If you have read any of his writings or listened to any of his tapes, he has always been a huge advocate of *"decision and focus."* All three words mean basically the same thing.

These are *"action"* words. These are *"thoughtform"* words. Assuming that we all trust the Law of Gravity, and although we may not have a scientific understanding of how it works, we have a general knowing, trust and belief of it simply working.

Chopra has said that stating an intention is an unseeable force, just like gravity. What if this is true? I happen to know by my own experience that it is true. Then we have the power of the *"sword in the stone."* We know how to remove the sword from the stone. It is with the power of intention.

Stating a pure intention, making a decision about something, simply makes it so. Do you believe that? Can you wrap your thoughts around that?

When you state an intention—and then just let it go—it happens. But many of us get in our own way by adding the word *"but—"* or we question, or we doubt.

A pure intent is with no wavering doubt. That is a mixed message to the Universe. Sometimes to get yourself out of that jam of negating your intention

---

[10] *Deepak Chopra materials can be found at any major bookstore. Any material used from him has been filtered through this author. (Audio) Creating Affluence, D. Chopra, 1993, New World Library.*

and not get caught up in the "hows" is to say, *"I have no idea how this is gonna work out, but I just trust that it does."* And if you are hit with another negating thought, you just un-negate it with that statement again. *"It will work out somehow."*

Many of my intentions have been placed around unknown things. Power to do things go beyond the norm. In order for me to accomplish this, I first have to rearrange my thinking.

Humans see all the steps necessary or what they think is necessary to accomplishing a goal. Spirit sees the end result. Period. Spirit sees the manifestation, the end result, period. We have to teach ourselves backwards of what we think we *"know."* Part of my own learning here is through intent. I simply intend to manifest as Spirit, and not as human. I am seeing it happen in some ways, and as I practice this, I simply get better at it.

But it has all started with an intention.

76

Thought Form=Action & Energy=Emotion

(by Susan James)

Part of our belief system, until it is not anymore, is that *"work=action=money/manifestation."* Within that is also that our desires manifest in the forms of opportunities and events. What we have forgotten is that an *"action"* can also be a *"thought form,"* and not something you have to physically go and do.

The test for us all is, can we have a thought form about a desire, and then let go of the desire quickly? There is an added element here as well. The thought form is the action, but the emotion attached to that thought form provides the energy, resulting in manifestation.

We can apply this to any area of our lives.

Thought form:	*I intend a relationship.*
Emotion:	*But I'll never have one.*
Thought form:	*I intend money.*
Emotion:	*But I'll never have any.*
Thought form:	*I intend health.*
Emotion:	*But I am unhealthy.*

The energy is in the emotion. That is where the manifestation takes place. You can feel the energy difference here:

Thought form:	*I intend a relationship.*
Emotion:	*This is wonderful to see how it unfolds!*

Thought form: *I intend money.*
Emotion: *Its coming from somewhere; who cares where!*

Thought form: *I intend health.*
Emotion: *I am getting better each day!*

There have been many things that I have had no idea how they would come about, but just trusted that somehow, someway, it would all work out. The *"trust"* that somehow, someway, is the *"emotion"* part applied to the *"thought-form"* (action).

It is always much easier to let go of things when you have peace that somehow it will just work out. You can dismiss the desire, and just let it go. If, however, you are carrying fear around a desire, then that fear is difficult to leave. You hang onto it for dear life. There is an ease in the emotion of letting go. There is a misery attached to fear, as it just grips onto you and appears to grow.

You have some additional help if you can't seem to let go of fears that lag along with your desires. You can ASK for peace over it. It does come. You can ask for your God/self or your Guides to help you dismiss the fear, and they will. There is always help. Just ASK!

77

The Wisdom Loft (Peace over Fear)

(by Susan James)

> **Question:** *How do I let go of gripping fear?*
> **Answer:** *Ask for peace over it.*
>
> **Question:** *Is it that simple to dismiss fear?*
> **Answer:** *Yes*
>
> **Question:** *What do I say, exactly?*
> **Answer:** *I now ask for peace over this fear/situation.*
>
> **Question:** *What if it comes back?*
> **Answer:** *Ask for peace over it.*

78

Ever Had a Teacher Give You the Answers?

(by Susan James)

I Student-taught my last Quarter in College. It was then I knew I did not want to teach in the present educational system. Luckily for me, I soon had a job lined up that paralleled my major, while others were sweating bullets, wondering if they would have any job, much less one in their field.

One of the deciding factors for me not to be a "teacher" in this was when I was to give a 6-week test to the class. I decided about a week before the test, to begin giving the class the answers to the test. I even told them that I was giving them the answers to the test. I said the question exactly as it would appear on the test, and gave the exact answer. All the while, I was also giving them pop quizzes, that I announced, so they weren't really "pop quizzes." And if they received 90% or above on each quiz, they would not have to take the six-weeks test.

Now, how blatantly easy is that? The down side was this: My supervising teacher did not like my method in the least. Major frowns from the back of the room and lectures on why I could not do that. It was just not done or appropriate behavior or example. But the "energy was in motion," so to speak, and the President of the University's daughter was in one of the classes, so it was a done deal, as far as I was concerned.

And why this story? What's my point? My point is this: We all have a Higher Self that already knows all of our answers, and our higher selves will give us the answers to our daily lives and needs and requirements and help our dreams come true—if we just ask. You just ask. But...

What if you have not yet developed an inner sense of knowing with your higher self. What if, what if, what if…?

It all begins with your desire level. This is how it works. Your Higher Self is like the teacher in front of your classroom. You have been told, "OK, guys, test time!"

And this is what can happen if you allow it, and you allow it by asking.

The really nice thing about this test is that you can ask for the answers.

You don't have to sweat and wonder: *Did I study enough?* Or *whoops, I forgot to study,* or *Hey, I didn't care enough to study.* This is like having your teacher in front of the class and you raise your hand, and you ASK her if she would please help you with the right answers, and she says, "Well yes, surely I will; that is what I am here for! I am here to give you all of the answers for the test!" And you say: "No Way!" And she says, "Yes, Way! The rules have changed! But you have to ask for the answers; I cannot volunteer them. Now that you know I am here and have recognized me, we can do this project together for your benefit and intended success, for I am your 'co-creative' partner, and together we will create wonder for your life and you will ACE this test!"

This teacher is your "higher self." Your higher self wants to give you the answers, and you get the answers by being clear in your questions.

It may help if we break down the definition of "question" so that this does not get in your way of clarity.

Other words for "question" are: matter, issue, request, asking, wondering. So, get clear in your matter of interest. Get clear on your issue. Get clear in your request. Get clear in your asking. Get clear on what you are really wondering about.

It helps with pen and paper in hand to just start writing. What is this that you really intend to happen? What is this that you are making a new decision and choice about? What are you wondering about, in regard to your current challenge or situation?

As you write, you become more clear. This happens because as you have one thought about an issue, you then have another, and the expansion of your subject matter grows. As it grows, so does your emoting/vibration. This is when the Universe now has information to work with. You have gotten clear in your "tone/vibration" by expanding your thoughts and feelings. Now the inspiration from the higher self begins, and you will feel it and know it.

As you are moving forward in "clarity," the answer "pops," seemingly out of nowhere. Then you have another choice, do you believe and act on the inspiration you just "think" you received? Well, do you?

79

Your Higher Self Has Your Answers, But…

(by Susan James)

Your Higher Self has your answers, but…Guess who is holding the Map to it all. You are, we are, I am. What is this map? It is your intuition and discernment.

Once again, your map, is your intuition and discernment.

Lets assume you have a question/pondering that you require an answer or "direction" on. You ask your Higher Self (teacher). Your HS gives you an answer, which helps you make a choice. But how do you "know" that the answer is the "correct" one, based on your intentions. Since you can't see your own future, how do you "know" that the inspiration/answer/direction that was given you is the "right" one?

You ask yourself how the answer that came to you "feels." Within your feeling lies your intuition and discernment. If you begin to "think" or "analyze" too long, you KILL the inspiration and you get confused and lose all clarity. It's like the answer got lost between you and the teacher somewhere in the aisle of confusion.

But one step further, as we begin to use the new energy gifts that are given us, we are protected from "error." I mean, how good is this? How good is God? How Good is Spirit?

As we begin to use our HS as our co-creative partners and state our intent, we almost become mistake-proof. Even if we "misdirect" ourselves, even if we don't quite follow through on the inspiration—out of lack of belief on some level, we are protected from our own error, and our HS makes sure that we get it "right," based on our intention.

Shoot, this is like you raise your hand, you ask the teacher for the answer. She tells you out loud, but you make an error and write down the wrong thing. She then walks over to your desk, takes your pencil from your hand, erases what you wrote, and in her own handwriting she writes the correct answer down on your own test paper. You just sit there, watching this all unfold before your eyes, and you go "Wow, this is so cool!"

Does it really happen like this? Is it really like this? Well, gee, this sounds like heaven or something.

And yes, dear ones, this is heaven, and it is all of ours now. Just by asking. But you have to ASK!

80

The Wisdom Loft (More Peace Over Fear)

(by Susan James)

Question: *This same fear keeps coming up. What should I do? Which "spiritual tool" should I use?*
Answer: *Ask for peace over it.*
Question: *Yes, but it keeps coming back.*
Answer: *Ask for peace over it.*
Question: *Can you please be more clear, so that I understand better how to use this peace tool for a fear that keeps coming back?*
Answer: *You have two choices.*

    1.   *You can attempt to "do" something or take an action from the place of fear, which will not give you either the solution or resolution you seek, OR*

    2.   *You can continue to ask for peace over it. If you are willing to ask for peace over an issue a 100 times per day, if necessary for you to have finally continued peace over a situation, then you will not only have peace, solution and resolution, but you will have "experience and knowing" in use of the "new energy spiritual tools" to apply to all areas of your life. This knowing of peace as a tool brings comfort and knowing and peace and ease. It is within peace that answers come, or shows up, or dissolves. If you have trouble believing in this as a tool, ASK for help to believe it and see it and use it.*

        When you are "willing" to ask for peace a 100 times over an issue, you never have to; it just goes away of its own weight. The Universe has heard your vibration and sincere desire for this to be the end of the fear. So be it.

Note: The detailed answer AFTER the question was finally asked with more clarity. Match/Match. Law of Attraction.

81

Amazing Things Happen in Flow

(by Susan James)

I began living my life "on purpose" about 5 years ago. That was a conscious decision. At that time, I had no idea or vision of what my purpose was, but I had placed my intent before I knew what I was really doing.

Since I had not found the area of my purpose to apply focus and creative energy to, I kept running into stuff, or stuff would run into me. None of it was bad, really, but since I had not yet known what vision and purpose was in my life, I still banged around a bit. I banged around because I was "vague" in my ASKING.

Little by little, as you have an over-all intention, the Universe starts stripping away the things that you no longer need so that you may realize your intent. Some of that stripping away comes in the forms of your physical, emotional, and spiritual world.

Some call it the "razors edge." You reach this point by dropping the stuff that will not contribute to your flow, so that you have no other choice but to do and be your vision and purpose. It is quite amazing when you see what has happened, and within that your own higher self, who knows more than your lower self, helps you to not mess it up for your personality "self."

When you have not yet established a vision for your life, it is difficult for you to have momentum carry you along. When you have momentum, that is when you feel the flow of life—of your life. I am there now.

My "there" means that I have momentum, that things show up that amaze me. Does this mean that I am now traveling the world on a lark? Not in this moment. That is not, however, my intent anyway. But what is happening is that I can watch my life from above and see that it is all unfolding perfectly for the "lark" to manifest with ease. In the meantime, there is no "meantime." I have finally gotten good at staying out of my own way.

For instance, I have stated in various writings that I see my computer as a "Christmas Gift Box," and that love and abundance flows from it. This happens to me every day. I get to do what I love to do, which brings me more of what I love to do, and it just gets bigger and better and happier.

I recently was led to make some new intentions for myself that came out of my wanting to know "more." That is one of my "constants"—more.

I have learned not to push anything. Wow, when you get here, the flow is so much better! My focus is crystal clear. I have always been good at focusing, but it has taken on a new look. A division of sorts has transpired within me.

What does this have to do with manifesting your stuff? Everything. My focus has brought me answers for my daily and future life that I had not yet thought of. My trust in my own wisdom, and knowing that I will bring me the answers that I need always, is more "security" than one could even think to beg for.

There is magic in my life, because I am willing to entertain all that I do not yet know. And with that, the Universe (which is really me) just sends me gifts on many levels.

In the beginning stages of my newsletter, I used to write a short piece on "Notice What You Notice." That has taken on a new level. I now see a person or event show up in my life and I know that this is attached to something that is about to happen in my NOW. Not tomorrow in my now, but like within the next little bit of my day. It's like I am in this maze (illusion), but I see from above, immediately, which turn to make or what is next around the immediate corner. As I write this, I just remembered that this is something that I "asked" for.

This is a little different from "synchronicity." The trick for me is "seeing" the event or person, and then have a knowing that in that moment this thing is about to happen. I have gotten good at watching my immediate now. I don't push. I don't take an action until it comes up right in front of me, and that's when I know to say "yes." I don't say "yes" too early or "no" too late. It is a skill—to get here. And which skill? ASKING. But not just "asking," asking with clarity.

No more guess work. I am simply shown ahead of time what is about to occur. This is part of momentum and flow.

One of the beginning ways to develop this is to "not react" or have a "knee jerk" response to events, small or large, as they show themselves.

This living life stuff is such a piece of art work. In the beginning, it looks like a "collage," and a mess of "which and what to do, and how?"

But then, as you ask for more knowing—and more understanding—your life begins to work like a fine-tuned orchestra; each piece and instrument is in tune with one another, and all events rise to bring you your fondest moments. It is a wonder to be here. I thank you for sharing this with me.

Susan

82

Thoughts, Thought Forms, Thresholds

(by Susan James)

As I have taken my own evolving seriously, and by "evolving" I mean "living heaven on earth," my "Asking" tends to be in high intent. I offer within the following paragraphs, three levels of thought of which, I have taught myself to use as tools to bring abundant flow to my life on new levels, physically as well as spiritually.

OK, here we go:

I define this in three steps:

1. Thought
2. Thought form
3. Threshold

1. **Thought** is there, always in our minds, running with no real purpose until we decide to direct it on purpose.

2. **Thought Form:** One way to direct it on purpose, more than just moving into a "positive mind set," is to ASK for a "new thought form." When you ask, it always comes. A new thought form is different from asking for guidance or direction. A new thought form is something that you have not thought about before. It gives you a new direction or new choice that you have not considered. It just pops into your mind, and you know. You have been deliberate and "clear" in asking for this "thought form" to bring you new information or choices that will fit in with your intent.

Lets say you need money to show up, and you don't know how or where. But maybe it's not the money; you need an extension for the money to show or a new resource so that you can keep something that you want to keep. You ask clearly for a new thought form, and then leave it. It won't be long and a "new idea" will show, and you will know your answer or action.

3. **Threshold:** I was moving through some barrier. I had not defined that barrier, but it was part of my Asking for "more." Something (I don't even remember what it was now) presented itself in the form of a major fear, and I had a sleepless night in fear for about three hours. I kept asking for peace over it, and that worked, but I had to ask for peace several times before I went to sleep. Then in the middle of the night, I felt a sensation in my brain. I woke up and the word "threshold" fell into my mind. That instantly told me that I had crossed a threshold that would now allow more of "something" to show up for me, and the energy around the fear I had would dissipate.

4. So I thought "Aha!" a new tool. So now if I have discovered some belief or barrier or wall or challenge that keeps popping up, but is disguised in a different situation, I know to now ask for a *new threshold*. It is best to ask for this in the form of an intention before going to sleep; that way your mind becomes a little more quiet, and it is easier for it to show. And if you are clear, it will show. Ask for it in ease. Don't forget that part. I had one or two agonizing nights because I forgot to ask for ease.

Sometimes you will just wake up out of a dead sleep, and you will know that you have "shifted." Sometimes you are given a word that tells you something, but you know it is a big thing. It is bigger than a Thoughtform, which is usually just intending over a specific issue. The threshold means that those same issues stop blocking you from your flow. One of the end results of this is that intentions that you have set for yourself come to you with momentum and ease, but more than that, you begin to "see" them coming before they arrive. Things really become fun when you are able to "see" it as this new level.

Susan

83

The Wisdom Loft

(by Susan James)

QUESTION: *If my life is ultimately about reaching "heaven on earth," what does that mean really for my "reality?"*

ANSWER: *"Heaven on Earth" becomes your reality.*

QUESTION: *Yes, but what does that mean?*

ANSWER: *What would "Heaven on Earth" mean to you? Therein lies your answer.*

Susan

84

The Trick to Getting What You Want

(By Susan James)

> *FACT:* *We flow energy.*
> *FACT:* *We flow energy with our thoughts and emotions.*
> *FACT:* *We flow energy either on purpose or not, but we flow energy, whether we know it or not.*

The TRICK to having things and experiences in our lives the way we "want them" is we MUST learn to "manipulate" HOW we flow this energy.

Simple exercise—and "Getting this" will break you of your old learned habits and give you more of what you want "faster."

> *YOU THINK:* *God/Universe, I want this! (Thing/condition/situation)*
> *UNIVERSE ANSWERS:* *YES...! YOU ARE "RIGHT!"*
>
> *YOU THINK:* *God/Universe, I want this, BUT it may not come.*
> *UNIVERSE ANSWERS:* *YES...! YOU ARE "RIGHT!"*

The trick is to "catch yourself" saying/thinking the BUT part. YOU KILL the creation. You launched the desire with your thought and good feeling about what you want, but then you KILL it with "BUT"...!

> *NOW...*
>
> *You Think/Say:* *God/Universe, I want this...!*
> *Universe Answers:* *YES!*

And You Say: ...*And this is what else I want, and I want it just because if feels good for me to have it! AND I WANT MORE!*

THIS IS MANIPULATING ENERGY TO CREATE/MANIFEST WHAT YOU WANT!

Daydream, daydream, daydream...*AND DON'T CHANGE YOUR MIND!*

Love Susan

85

The Law of Attraction... Works...
The Law of Manifesting... Works...

(by Susan James)

"Give your full attention to your desire. Give it your full and undivided attention, and if you are giving your full and undivided attention, then you are in vibrational harmony with your desire and the Universe has to give you your desire."

"BUT—most of you don't do that. When you have contrast (negative desire/emotion), you give birth to your desire, BUT you give more attention to the contrast, than the Desire."

"IF you pay more attention to the contrast, THAT IS WHAT YOU GET!"

"IF you pay more attention to the Desire, THAT IS WHAT YOU GET!"

This is the Law of Attraction. It works. Period.

You are flowing energy. Period.

You are either flowing energy towards what you want—or what you do not want. Period.

TEACH YOURSELF THE LAW OF ATTRACTION AND THEN YOU WON'T NEED TO HAVE FAITH; YOU WILL HAVE "KNOWLEDGE" THAT WHAT YOU FOCUS ON WILL BE. (Abraham-Hicks)

Love Susan

86

Do You Want to Get Your Dream Back?

(by Susan James)

Due to the nature of this book, I am able to make some assumptions. You most likely are a "free spirited" type of person, maybe an entrepreneur, if not in your livelihood presently, a secret yearning.

You most likely have read books and articles with someone making the comment that we lose our desires and dreams along the way of our adult "doing" thing.

I am here to tell you that is hogwash.

Since I have been actively participating in the wonder cyberworld, I have found that folks very much have dreams and desires and wants, and they come from all walks of life and financial status.

They all still have dreams. What they want is hope, but more than hope, they want to believe that it can happen for them.

But they don't know where to go for this hope, and if they find the hope, what next? What do I "do?" If I get my dream back, what do I "do" next?

The answer is "nothing," you do not "do" anything until you "feel" like it.

We are so conditioned and taught that the next step is always to DO!

If you have been paying attention at all to any of the essays so far, you have to know that it all has to do with "how you feel."

Don't do anything until you feel like it, until you can't help BUT to do something.

Feel something, feel something good, then do; don't do first, *THAT IS BACK-WARDS!*

You've read here, of a wonderful woman who used the application of Universal Law and Energy to Manifest her dream home within a year. What was the major Element contributing to that happening? **DESIRE.** It all started with **DESIRE!**

So, my dear ones, what do you want if you really could have "things your way," how would it be? **WRITE IT DOWN!** Then notice how you feel while you are writing it down. That is your Divinity guiding you!

Dream on!

Love Susan

87

Inside the Box vs. Outside the Box

(by Susan James)

> **INSIDE THE BOX**
> Is always been this way.
> He should not do it that way,
> But they said that
> We just don't do it that way;
> It's a fact of life.
> Don't be so loud,
> You're acting like a 2-year-old.
> The Book says you can't do that.
> I'm from here, so I can't get there.

OUTSIDE THE BOX
Wow! I didn't even know this stuff was here!
Look at how much fun it is here!
All are welcome here!
I can do anything I really want to do here!
I feel this incredible sense of freedom here!
This is so *GRAND*! What if I never knew it was like this?

What took you so long to come "outside the box?"

Well, they told me "inside the box" was were I "belonged," and not to dare go to the land "outside the box…" You never know what can happen…

So how did you finally get here, to the land "outside the box?"

Someone loved me enough to bring me here.

88

What is a Vortex, and What Does It Have to Do with Your Desires?

(by Susan James)

Picture yourself as a cyclone, having that whirlpool kind of action, just sucking up everything within its path. You, as this cyclone, are extremely focused. You are in one area, and you are pulling into you anything and everything around you.

You, as this vortex, cyclone are full of powerful energy—energy that you can point towards things that you want, or things that you do not want.

So what does this vortex, cyclone, have to do with your desires? You have to make a decision about what you want so you have the force of nature (Universe) at your whim.

Once you make a decision and know in your heart that you will not be denied this intention, that desire takes on the effect of a cyclone. It creates a "vortex" between you and the Universe. The Universe/God, helps you in this energy, BUT it can only help you by your making the first step. And the first step is in *DECISION*.

Have you created a Vortex to bring power to your Desires, so that the Law of Attraction brings to you what you have decided that you choose to have?

If you have not, what is it going to take? More of the same stuff that you do not want until you just cannot take it anymore? You do not have to wait until the "other shoe drops" to make a decision. Oh, you can, but you have the tools, to bring your desires to you *NOW*, without going through the *agony* first!

This is what a Vortex has to do with your desires.

It makes them Powerful!

Love Susan

89

When They Ask

(by Susan James)

Okay, I have a very good friend; we've been friends for almost 15 years. When she asks me "What are you doing?" I make a stab at explaining it to her, and she gets this "blank" look on her face. Now this girl loves me, so it is a supportive blank, different from others who "also love me" but have no tolerance for what I tell them.

This friend is married, has four children, works, and does all the other stuff that busy moms have to do. So when I generalize some of the stuff that I do and she gives her blank stare, she goes, "I just don't get it. How do people have time for the Internet stuff?" Her high school aged son, has to print out any E-mail she may get, which is none almost, and she walks around trying to read it as she is doing the other busy stuff of her life.

So why do I tell you this?

Because you and I have a responsibility, as we learn how to use the Laws of the Universe, as we make our lives easier and more abundant in all areas, we are the ones, the ones who are attracted to this information and make huge leaps in integrating it into our lives. We have to be gentle with our friends and neighbors—oh, yes, and the relatives—and when they begin asking, because they will, we have to be ready…

Are you ready?

Love Susan

90

Un-Stucking to Move Forward

(by Susan James)

I had been stuck on a definition.

Some of the inspired readings that I absolutely soak up use the word "sustenance."

I was "stuck" because my definition of the word was "only at the point of need," and this just did not fit for me at all, and it was giving me a challenge.

The "thing" I have taught myself to do is when something feels like that to me, then it means there is something new for me to learn; if I just "ask" for the information to come to me, then it will, and it ALWAYS does.

Of course the answer came. It, of course, was simple, but as many times, we are so much in the "challenge" that we cannot "see" straight, as it was for me in this case.

The answer was: I needed to change my definition, my belief, around the word "sustenance."

As soon as I "realized" that, my understanding again grew in leaps and bounds, but along with that, another example of "ask and you shall receive."

Please, if you want/choose/intend/desire more in any area of your life—you gotta ASK!

Love Susan

91

The Basics of Feeling Good: Getting Back There

(by Susan James)

Long story short: I've gotten good at this "deliberate creation" stuff. I am in joy, bliss, yada most of the time, and my life runs very smoothly and is filled with passion for what I do. I very seldom have a "low energy" day, and when I do, it feels like WHAM!

I had one of those one Sunday, and the whole time I was feeling crummy, good things were still happening for me, so it was funny, sorta, that I could not pull myself out of this "thing." I could not move forward on the projects I was intending for—

I just felt crummy.

So, the next morning, out came the ammunition. The good ole basics that had gotten me to this place that I am in—PLUS, since by that time I had read six Kryon books, my Guides are an integral part of my process. So I began telling them, "you guys have to help pull me out of this," and I told them the same thing the next morning morning.

So I combined my Basic "Abraham" motto of "The most important thing I can do is to feel good," along with the 9-3-9 exercise from Jeane Marshalls Website, which is I write 9 times with my dominant hand "I feel good," and then 3X with my non-dominant hand, "I feel good" and then repeat 9X "I feel good," (dominant). I was cured in less than 10 minutes! It was then early here in VA, and I am was on a roll already.

I did the 9–3–9 exercise before coming to the office, and the last song on the radio as I was about to shut off my car was "I Feel Good!" James Brown—Law of Attraction at its best, with the pure assistance of my guides.

I go into length here, because sometimes I forget how "low" low can feel, and for those just beginning to work with the new energy and the Laws of the Universe, or the folks who have been around this a while, we all, including me, can always use a reminder of how to get back to that "place." That place that is crucial to that stream of all good things coming to us. That place of "feeling good, no matter what!" Have an incredible day! Celebrate This Life!

Love Susan

Afterword

This book is pure Manifesting of My Dream Come True. I thank you for reading the words and taking what felt good to you, into your heart.

My own growth and continued applications of "knowings" became quite clear in my own editing of the information presented within these pages.

For most of us, getting what we want is really simply attached to having a commitment or vision of our lives, which can be as simple as joy and happiness. The rest are the actual tools and instruments, which come in the disguise of livelihoods, families, desires, choices and evolving beliefs, which is what we use to provide the energy to get us "there."

We can get there the hard way or the easy way. It's easier and faster if you continually ASK. By asking, which is a desire, you are brought the information to fulfill that. Our job then is to "watch and listen " for the signs on the path, for they are given.

In my asking, which has led to this publication, it led me to folks who helped me get here. I have a special thanks to extend to David Gordon, who moderates an interactive list related to Abraham-Hicks. It was there that I began pounding away at my self in a deliberate manner. It was there that I honed my skills of thinking "on purpose," of manifesting with deliberate thought.

To Sharon Gladson, whom when I first began the Newsletter series, entered my life and carried ads for the newsletter free of charge in her own growing publication.

Also, to Kristen Fox, whose wisdom is offered in this book. Kristen has been extremely supportive of my writings through her own care of me, her various Web-sites and similar publications.

And then there is Trixi Summers. As I have told her many times, there are no words to describe her contribution to my growth and evolving. She has been the one who has helped me to reach clarity and pureness. And from this place, wonder flows towards me.

This newsletter series, now in book form, was made possible by many hearts continuing towards their own joy. This also included Michele Johnson, the orginial publisher of this in ebook form, who saw something in my writing and suggested we do something together, and now here we are.

Many have helped me build my dream, and I am thankful. The rest of the story and taking Manifesting further into the beyond stage, continues to expand as I do. My expansion shows in more books, consulting, courses, and speaking engagements. Please visit my website to see what the application of User Friendly Physics has done for my own life! (http://www.susanjames.org)

Have a good time; it's why you came! Susan James

Contributions, Resources, Acknowledgments

The Following Contributions, Resources and Acknowledgments are part of the energies that have contributed to the development of my own heart and the Manifesting 101 series:

9–3–9 Exercise

This exercise was paraphrased from the Web-site of Jeanie Marshall, Empowerment Consultant, Marshall House, P.O.Box 918, Santa Monica, CA 90406.

http://www.mhmail.com A great site!

17 Seconds and other Deliberate Creation information including, but not limited to, Laws of Deliberate Creation, Attraction and Allowing, "The Basis of Life is Freedom, The Objective of Life is Joy, The Result of Live is Growth" (Abraham, 1989) © Abraham-Hicks Publications Jerry & Esther Hicks P.O.Box 690070, San Antonio, Texas 78269

http://www.abraham-hicks.com

"The Ultimate Secret to Getting Absolutely Everything You Want" by Mike Hernacki. (Accelerating Acceleration) (book) Berkley Books, 200 Madison Ave, NY, NY 10016

"Blueprint for Change" by Darryl Anka Bashar Communications, 1920 North Lake Avenue, Suite 108 Altadena, CA 91001 http://www.bashartapes.com

ABE (notations from Sharon Hackleman's House Story) Laws of Deliberate Creation, Attraction and Allowing, "The Basis of Life is Freedom, The Objective of Life is Joy, The Result of Life is Growth" (Abraham, 1989) © Abraham-Hicks Publications, Jerry & Esther Hicks, P.O. Box 690070, San Antonio, Texas 78269 http://www.abraham-hicks.com.

Resource for:

"How Do You Enter the Door of Abundance"
New vs. Old Energy, The Chair, The Kryon Papers, Partnering with God
The Kryon Papers, Self Worth+Peace=Abundance
Discussion of the New Energy and the Handshake with Spirit
Discussion of the New Energy, Intent and Map
The Kryon Papers Books 1–7 by Lee Carroll
The Kryon Writings, Inc., PMB 422/1155, Camino Del Mar, Del Mar, CA 92014
The Kryon Papers (Lee Carroll) http://www.kryon.com

Ascended Masters: Christ Consciousness *http://www.lord-maitreya.org*

Biographies

William Wayne Barnes, (pen name), began his career in 1975 as a high school language teacher. He holds Bachelor of Arts degrees from The Cleveland State University in Spanish, Italian, secondary education and music. In 1979, he moved to Washington, D.C.. In 1993 he and his wife, Mary Ann, moved to Arizona, where they raise poultry and exotic birds. Although his Titanic odyssey began when he was a toddler, it was not until age 44 that he truly opened himself up to the possibilities of reincarnation. Since that time, William Wayne Barnes has taken on the mission to tell the Thomas Andrews' story, and to search out and assist others who, like himself, have been troubled by past-life memories. http://www.titanicmemories.8m.com/main.html

Kristen Fox: I'm an Artist, Writer, and Conscious Creator. My partner John and I are constantly investigating and honing our abilities to consciously create-and together we share our journeys through a number of websites. The Conscious Creation website offers an introduction to reality creation, hundreds of articles in the Conscious Creation Journal, sessions of practical channeled reality creation information, an e-mail discussion list and more! (http://www.consciouscreation.com) John's Parabolic Mirror site offers semi-daily insights on current events and personal experiences as seen through the eyes of a conscious creator. (http://www.parabolicmirror.com) And my art shop contains conscious creation and metaphysical, Celtic, and humorous t-shirts, mugs, posters, etc and is constantly expanding. (http://shop.foxvox.org) Why wait-go create!

Tom Haskins is one of the highest-rated instructors at a college in Denver, where he has been teaching since 1992. In that time, he has also read over 600 books to answer the questions that stayed with him from experiences as a licensed architect, management consultant, corporate trainer and educational materials developer. He is currently designing a web site that will support people in manifesting successful endeavors and supportive relationships. Tom can be reached by E-mail at *haskins@ecentral.com*

Carol James is a visionary, writer, teacher, coach, mentor and founder of Inspired Living website (http://www.inspiredinside.com.) She publishes the "Inspired Lifestyles Newsletter," and is co-developer of the Transformative

Thinking (tm) technology, which is detailed in the Transformative Thinking: Your Road to Self-Empowerment.

Jeri Noble has been a professional counselor for over 25 years in a variety of modalities. These include past life regression therapy, astrology and as a metaphysical practitioner. Jeri lives with her life partner, Tom, (that's right, Tom and Jeri) and their dog, Silky, in the New Age mecca: Sedona, Arizona. An avid bookworm and writer, she produces several weekly columns, plus original weekly articles for her Web-site, Circles of Light. (http:www.//circlesoflight.com)

John Welsh is a Chicago native, currently enjoying life in the Lakeview area of Chicago. Involved in metaphysical pursuits since 12 years old, John has discovered where the human potential lies mostly—in the mind and spirit. His current projects include developing a program of study to develop our higher mental functions, and also creating more commercial applications for the use of psychic ability.

Never Ending and Always Beginning

Susan James
www.susanjames.org

0-595-14414-4

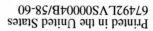

Printed in the United States
67492LV S00004B/58-60